For A, K & L.

CONTENTS

# Introduction

Wellbeing I won
And wisdom too,
And grew and joyed in my growth
From a word to word
I was led to a word
From a deed to another deed.

It was these words, sound-tracked by crows and a distant tolling bell, that began my journey towards The Hávamál. I heard them on a friends' mix-tape and the phrases intrigued me for months. I proceeded to copy the thirty-six second track onto my own mix-tapes and eventually learned that it was taken from the intro to a thrash album by the British band Sabbat[1].

It was many years later when I learned that the words were not an original poem, but a verse from an obscure translation of a 13th century Icelandic text. H. A. Bellows gives the title as "The Hovamol", other translators have opted for 'The Sayings of Har' or sometimes 'The Sayings of the High One'. It is most commonly referred to as "The Hávamál".

# Historical Background

The Hávamál, is the second poem of The Poetic (or Elder) Edda, an anonymous collection of poems written in Old Norse. The Poetic Edda enters recorded history in 1643CE as part of the Codex Regius a forty-five vellum[2] leaf collection in the possession of Brynjólfur Sveinsson, the Bishop of Skálholt. Despite this late date there is circumstantial evidence that The Hávamál was composed much earlier.

---

[1] "Dreamweaver – Reflections of our Yesterdays" (Noise, 1989). It was heavily influenced by Brian Bates novel "The Way of Wyrd", that deals with the clash of Christianity and Anglo-Saxon paganism in early Britain.

[2] Calf-skin parchment - Latin "vitulinum", Old French "vélin" (calfskin).

The possibility of an earlier composition, is found in the first verse of "The Gylfaginning", from the Prose Edda. This collection often called The "Younger" Edda was composed by Snorri Sturluson as a guide to the poetical styles and has been dated c.1220CE. The opening verse from The Hávamál is used without interpolation or adjustment by the protagonist Gylfi. He speaks the words, ostensibly as a piece of guidance to himself, upon entering an unfamiliar hall. This does suggest it was already sufficiently known by this date as to require no explanation to its audience.

| | |
|---|---|
| Gáttir allar, | All the gateways |
| áðr gangi fram, | ere one goes out |
| um skyggnask skyli, | Should one scan: |
| því at óvíst er at vita | For 'tis uncertain |
| hvar óvinir sitja | where sit the unfriendly |
| á fleti fyrir. | On the bench before thee. |

- Gylfaginning

The Hávamáls date of composition may be even earlier. Eyvindr 'The Plagiarist', also includes one of The Hávamáls more famous verses in the final verse of his "Hákonarmál" (The Lay of King Hákon the Good). This text has been dated three centuries earlier to c960CE:

| | |
|---|---|
| Deyr fé, | Cattle die, |
| deyja frændr | kinsmen die, |
| eyðisk land ok láð. | land and sea are destroyed. |
| Síz Hákon fór | Since Hákon left |
| með heiðin goð, | with heathen[3] gods |
| mǫrg es þjóð of þéuð. | many people are oppressed.[4] |

- Verse 22, Hákonarmál

[3] A significant early use of the word *heiðin* (heathen) see Abram (2011).

[4] Older translations have "...ever since Hákon, to the heathen gods fared,"

Eyvindr may have simply been copying, as his nickname suggests, or it may be that this concept was a well known Norse proverb to his intended audience. Regardless of its provenance, it is a clearly a paraphrase of what is one of the more famous verses in The Hávamál:-

| | |
|---|---|
| Deyr fé | Cattle die, |
| deyja frændr | and kinsmen die, |
| deyr sjálfr it sama | And so one dies one's self; |
| ek veit einn | One thing now |
| at aldri deyr | that never dies, |
| dómr um dauðan hvern | fame of a dead man's deeds. |

- Verse 76, The Hávamál

Although it is likely that the Hákonarmál borrowed from The Hávamál - it is also possible that both are drawing from a third unknown source.

One unusual view on the origin of The Hávamál is that of Klaus von See, who interprets the text solely as a product of the post-conversion era. His theory is that The Hávamál is an alternate, lesser, version of the "Catonis Distichia" (Distichs of Cato), with some interpolations from The Hugsvinnsmál.

The Distichs of Cato is an anonymous Roman text, attributed to the otherwise undistinguished Dionysius Cato (and sometimes, erroneously to Cato the Elder, author of "The Republic"). It has been dated to the 3rd or 4th century CE, and was well known in the Middle Ages as a school-book for instruction in Latin and ethics. The Hugsvinnsmál (The Speech of the Wise Minded One) is a more obvious Old Norse translation of the Distichs of Cato and usually comprises 148 verses or strophes.

Despite the number of similarities, the current academic position is stated best by John McKinnel. He disputes any influence of Cato, arguing persuasively, that The Hugsvinnsmál is more likely to have been influenced by The Hávamál.[5] He also concludes that there is "little to support von See's argument" for the Distichs of Cato theory.

## Other Sources

The Hávamál clearly resonated with the people of the Viking era diaspora and their subsequent descendants, and echoes of it have been found in the most unusual of circumstances.

Although Orkney is fortunate in that some of its texts have been preserved such as the "Orkneyinga saga" which recalls the events beginning in the ninth century, it is the rarer Shetland evidence that is most intriguing.

| | |
|---|---|
| Nine days he hang | Nine days he hung |
| pa da rootless tree, | on the Rootless Tree; |
| For ill was da fők | For bad was the folk, |
| an göd was he; | and good was he |
| A blöddy met was in his side, | A bloody mark was in his side- |
| Made wi a lance | Made with a lance |
| at widna hide; | that would not hide[6] |
| Nine lang nicht | Nine long nights, |
| i da nippin rime | in the nipping rime, |
| Hang he dere | Hung he there |
| wi his naked limb, | with his naked limb. |
| Some dey leuch | Some, they laughed; |
| Bit idders grett. | But others wept. |

- "Unst Lay" Fragment (trans. Karl Blind)

[5] McKinnels 'Essays on Eddic Poetry' is an in depth analysis of a number of ancient sources, and explores the maze of similarities and interpolations between The Distichs of Cato, The Hugsvinnsmál and The Hávamál.

[6] heal

A VSNR[7] researcher recorded this fascinating fragment, known as the "*Unst Lay*" in 1865 from a so-called 'wise-woman' in Shetland. The poem is a sort-of Christianized update of the first verse of "*Rúnatáls þáttr Óðins*" (Odins Rune Song). The poem was later analysed by folklorist Karl Blind in Volume I of the VSNR Saga Book and also in an expanded, stand-alone article.

Blind makes the point that "the aged woman who recited the eight lines was quite aware that that they could not strictly apply to Christ [and s]he knew in what points they differed from the Biblical statement. [But m]ore than the fragment of eight lines she did not remember."

Compare the following:

| | |
|---|---|
| Veit ek at ek hekk | I know that I hung, |
| vindga meiði á | on a wind-rocked tree, |
| nætr allar níu | nine whole nights, |
| geiri undaðr | with a spear wounded, |
| ok gefinn Óðni | and to Óðinn offered, |
| sjálfr sjálfum mér | myself to myself; |
| á þeim meiði | on that tree, |
| er manngi veit | of which no one knows |
| hvers hann af rótum renn | from what root it springs. |

- Verse 138, The Hávamál

As Blind points out, that while the verse has been heavily adapted, though effort has been made to maintain the rhyming structure, presumably as an aid to memorizing.

---

[7] The huge interest in folklore in the 19th century led to the creation of The Viking Society for Northern Research (VSNR), an institution that persists to this day. Its broad ranging remit was to document the archaeology and existing anthropological oral traditions of Shetland and the Orkney Isles.

The survival of the text as an oral tradition[8], however fragmentary, in a non-literate society 1000 years after the Christian conversion era is testament to its the cultural importance. This cultural significance may also explain why The Hávamál was first recorded five centures earlier.

## Gnomic Verse

Regardless of its origins, what is certain, is that the The Hávamál firmly belongs in that genre known as gnomic poetry. The word 'gnome'[9] here is a word that finds its antecedents in 18th century French with "*gnomique*" a word borrowed from the Latin "*gnomicus*"(concerned with maxims). The Latin is in turn derived from the Greek γνώμη "*gnome*" (thought, judgement), and related cognates such as γιγνώσκειν "*gignoskein*" (to know) and γνώμικός "gnōmikós".

The idea has been applied to writings found in ancient literatures as disparate as the Seven Sages of Ancient Greece

> γνῶθι σεαυτόν,
> gnothi seauton (Know thyself.)
> - Attributed to Thales of Miletus

And the "*De duodecim abusivis saeculi*" (On the Twelve Abuses of the World) an 8th century anonymous text which condemns the following:

---

[8] It is tempting to imagine the Hávamál as a Ritual Drama (with call and response?), but as yet there is insufficient evidence to support this. Although Price and Mortimer (2004) argue that, the wearer of the Sutton Hoo helmet was seen as both war leader and war god, a literal personification of Odin.

[9] The word gnome, in this case, does not refer to the creatures of High Renaissance magic as described by Paraclesus. The latin root "*gnomus*" or "*gnomi*" may be a corruption of the greek Πυγμαῖοι "*pygmaioi*" (pygmy).

| | |
|---|---|
| *sapiens sine operibus* | *the wise man without works* |
| *senex sine religione* | *the old man without religion* |
| *adolescens sine oboedientia* | *the young man without obedience* |
| *dives sine elemosyna* | *the rich man without charity* |
| *femina sine pudicitia* | *the woman without modesty* |
| *dominus sine virtute* | *the nobleman without virtue* |
| *Christianius contentiosus* | *the argumentative Christian* |
| *pauper superbus* | *the proud pauper* |
| *rex iniquus* | *the unjust king* |
| *episcopus neglegens* | *the neglectful bishop* |
| *plebs sine disciplina* | *the community without order* |
| *populus sine lege* | *the people without a law* |

This sort of advice is common in many of the texts and treatises of the period, and was by no means confined to Christian cultural mores.

Another notable wisdom text from this era is "*Tecosca*[10] *Cormaic*" (The Instructions of Cormac) written in Old Irish and attributed to the High-King, Cormac mac Airt. This short text has been dated to the early ninth century and takes the form of an instructional dialogue between Cormac and his son Coirpre[11].

Note the similarities between the treatment of guests in The Hávamál:

| | |
|---|---|
| "A húi Chuind, a | "O Cormac, grandson of Conn", |
| Chormaic," ol Carpre | said Coipre, |
| "cadeat ada flatha | "what are the dues of a chief and an |
| cuirmthige?" | ale-house?" |
| "Ní hansam," ol Cormac. | "Not hard to tell", said Cormac |
| "Costud im daglaith, | "Good behavior around a good chief, |
| Lassamna do lochrannaib, | Lights to lamps |

[10] Also "Teagasca".

[11] Some translators prefer Carbre or Carbery

| | |
|---|---|
| Luthbas im ṡochaide, | Exerting oneself for the company |
| Samugud suide, | A proper settlement of seats |
| Soichlige dáleman, | Liberality of dispensers, |
| Díanlám oc fodail, | A nimble hand at distributing |
| Fochraibe oc timthirecht, | Attentive service |
| Tigerna do charthain, | To love one's lord, |

- Tecosca Cormaic (trans. Kuno Meyer)

Although it is tempting to draw parallels with The Hávamál, it is more likely that this treatment of guests reflects a broader tradition found in many European cultures of the time.[12]

Certainly "cuirmthige" (tavern) is referred to in the previous century as something which should belong to a Rí (King or Chieftain)[13] but may also have been a place where ale was brewed and sold for consumption. Sold in this case may refer to the brewer being subsidized by the local "Rí"[14], so the name may simply be the location of a professional brewer.

Actual examples of the Old Irish word "*midchúarto*" (mead-hall) can be found linked with advice to speak plainly:

| | |
|---|---|
| "Ní ba gerthude i | "Let him not be greasy[15] |
| n-ailt midchúarto" | in the mead-hall" |

- (ibid, Section 3)

---

[12] Although gnomic in style, *Tecosca Cormaic*, is more properly part of the 'Mirrors for Princes' genre. e.g. *De Clementia* by Seneca or 道德經 (Dao De Jing) attributed to 老子 (Lao Tzu) as well as the fragmentary early Wallachian text "*Neagoe Basarab, Învăţăturile lui Neagoe Basarab către fiul său Theodosie*" (The teachings of Neagoe Basarab to his Son Theodosius). Machiavellis "*Il Principe*" (The Prince) is atypical.

[13] See "*Crith Gablach*" (Branded purchase) an Old Irish Law book from c700CE, although Nelson (Routledge 2005) dates it to the 5th Century CE.

[14] Ancient Gaelic designation for one of the three ranks of King

[15] Slippery, untruthful, from "*gerthide*" (suety, fatty).

And the most pertinent etymological reference about the qualities of a chief:

| | |
|---|---|
| "Cest, caté téchta flatha?" | "Question, what are the proper |
| ol Carpre. | qualities of a chief",said Coipre. |
| "Ní hansam," ol Cormac. | "Not hard to tell", said Cormac |
| ... | ... |
| rop griam | let him be the sun of |
| tige midchúarto." | the mead-hall." |

-(ibid, Section 6)

The key Old Irish phrase here is "*tige midchúarto*", where "*tige*" is a form of "*tech*" (house or dwelling, moden Irish "*teach*"). The phrase is also related to the "*teach midchúarta*" at Tara which is often rendered as 'House of Mead-circling'. This sort of building would probably have been more synonymous with Anglo-Saxon institutions, with the local *Rí* holding court there at least part-time.

The Hill of Tara is also linked with "*Medb Lethderg*" (Maeve Red-side), a goddess who was wife or lover of nine successive kings, (including *Cormac mac Airt*). This repeated relationship and the meaning of "*Medb*" as 'she who intoxicates' suggests a ritualistic and etymological link to the drink mead. The ancient form of honey wine has religious connotations in many cultures and was often consumed during a marriage ceremony. This confluence of meanings have been interpreted as ritual; symbolic marriages to confer sacral Kingship[16] in the perceived 'ancestral' mead-hall of Tara.

---

[16] Dexter, Miriam Robbins. "*Indo-European Reflections of Virginity and Autonomy.*" Mankind Quarterly, 26 (1–2): 57–74 (Fall/Winter 1985)

## A Sacred Text

The Hávamál, although not explicitly religious, has had a profound influence on modern neo-paganism and the modern religious movement collectively referred to as Heathenry. It was certainly one of the main inspirations for the development of the Heathen 'creeds' such as "The Nine Noble Virtues" or "The Six Fold Goal". The origin and authorship of these bullet-points has been claimed by John Yeowell and John Gibbs-Bailey of the Odinic Rite, and also by Stephen A. McNallen of the Asatru Folk Assembly. A futher view is that the list was compiled by Stephen Flowers when he was a member of the Asatru Free Assembly.

These intial developments are now seen as a first step, rather than an enduring creed in modern heathenry. Particularly in a developing religion where scholarship as well as orthopraxy are increasingly viewed as more important.

So the Hávamál seems to have taken on a life of its own independent of its unknown creators and compilers. Although perhaps begun as a collection of mottos and maxims, it has since become partly synonymous with Asatru and Heathenry. Each new generation finding increasing worth in its compact guidance and intimations; perhaps unconsciously taking Cicero's etymological origin for the word religion as being from "relegere" - to re-read or go over a text.

## This Edition

The compact nature of Old Norse and its use of kennings presents a significant problem not just for the translator, but also for modern readers. It is for this reason, that this edition presents three different translations of the text, side-by-side with Old Norse. However to maintain this approach throughout the text, it has been necessary to adjust the verse order from the original published English translation.

Old Norse – For this edition the standardised Old Norse has been used. It was Sophus Bugge who transcribed and emended the unusual spellings, abbreviations and other orthographic quirks of the original text. His work was further standardized by later scholars as can be seen in this example from Verse 138.

| | | | | | | |
|---|---|---|---|---|---|---|
| **Codex Regius** | | gefi | Oðni | sialfr | sialf | m |
| **Bugge** | oc | gefinn | Oðni, | sialfr | sialfrom | mer |
| **Standardisation** | ok | gefinn | Oðni, | sjálfr | sjálfum | mér |

Thorpe - Benjamin Thorpe was an Anglo-Saxon scholar, but in 1866 he published one of the first modern English translations of the Hávamál.

Bellows - Henry Adams Bellows is the most recent translation, The Poetic Edda, 1936, “Hovamol: The Ballad of the High One”

Bray - Although lesser known, Olive Brays 1908 edition of the text still has some intriguing approaches to the wordplay of the original.

## Other Translations

Auden, W.H. & Taylor, P.B. – The poet and an academic who published selections from the Poetic Edda, in 1969.

Beinteinsson, Sveinbjörn - The leader of the Icelandic Ásatrúarfélagið, recorded an album of of Eddaic poems, including the Hávamál, chanted in rímur style[17]

Chisholm, James Allen – The author was a founder member, first Steersman and current Elder Emeritus of the United States heathen organization 'The Troth' (formerly 'The Ring Of Troth').

Crawford, Jackson - The Cowboy Hávamál by Crawford began as a joke but its popularity led to the author including it in recent editions of his own regular translation of The Poetic Edda.

Dronke, Ursula - This translation of the Edda, has been highly praised within academia as a balance of linguistic accuracy with poetic phrasing.

Hollander, Lee M. - Another translation of the Hávamál can be found in Hollanders 1928 editon of The Poetic Edda. The author was also an Honorary life member of the VSNR.

Larrington, Dr. Carolyne - A supernumerary fellow, and tutor in medieval English literature at St. John's College, Oxford. Her translation was first published in 1996.

Terry, Patricia - Published in 1969, this translation of The Poetic Edda was also released in 2015 as an audiobook. ThomaS Landbo's Danish inflection on his narration of The Hávamál is certainly worth seeking out.

---

[17] A traditional poetic style for epic (and informal) poetry using one of four specific diatonic melodic scales - rímnalög, kvæðalög, stemmur

## Bibliography

Abram, Christopher (2011). *Myths of the Pagan North: The Gods of the Norsemen.* New York: Continuum International Publishing Group.

Blind, K. "Discovery of Odinic Songs in Shetland" (1879)

Blind, K. "*Shetland Folklore and the Old Faith of the Scandinavians and Teutons*", Saga Book Vol. I, Viking Society for Northern Research (1892)

Dexter, Miriam Robbins. "Indo-European Reflections of Virginity and Autonomy." Mankind Quarterly, 26 (1–2): 57–74 (Fall/Winter 1985)

Evans, David A. H. (ed) *Text Series Volume VII: Hávamál*, Viking Society for Northern Research, (1986)

Fomin M., A Newly Discovered Fragment of the Early Irish Wisdom Text Tecosca Cormaic in TCD MS 1298 (H. 2. 7)

Meyer, K., ed., *Tecosca Cormaic. The Instructions of King Cormaic Mac Airt*, RIA Todd Lecture Series 15, Dublin: RIA, 1909.

McKinnel, J. eds Kick, D & Shafer, J. D. *Essays on Eddic Poetry,* University of Toronto Press, 2014

Nelson, M., The Barbarian's Beverage: A History of Beer in Ancient Europe, Routledge 2005

North, R., Allard, J., Gillies, P., Longman Anthology of Old English, Old Icelandic, and Anglo Norman Literatures, Routledge, 2014.

Pollington, S., *The Mead Hall*, Anglo-Saxon Books, 2003

Price, Neil & Mortimer, Paul. "*An Eye for Odin? Divine Role-Playing in the Age of Sutton Hoo*". European Journal of Archaeology. European Association of Archaeologists. 17 (3): 517–538 (2004)

Rood, J., Nordvig, M., Walker, M., Wills, J., Lacharity, E., Linzie, B. (eds) *Óðroerir: The Heathen Journal Volume II.* 2012

Pulsiano P., *Medieval Scandinavia: An Encyclopedia*, Taylor & Francis, 1993

Vermeers C. L., Teagasca: The Instructions of Cormac Mac Airt, Faoladh Books, 2014

Vigfusson G., Powell, F Y (eds) Corpus Poeticum Boreale V1, Eddic Poetry: The Poetry Of The Old Northern Tongue, From The Earliest Times To The Thirteenth Century (1883), Kessinger Publishing, 2010

Von See, K., *Disticha Catonis und Hávamál*, Paul und Braunes Beiträge, 1972

# The Hávamál

| Verse | Old | Gáttir allar |
|---|---|---|
| 1 | Norse | áðr gangi fram |
| | | um skoðask skyli, |
| | | um skyggnast skyli, |
| | | því at óvíst er at vita |
| | | hvar óvinir sitja |
| | | á fleti fyrir. |
| | Thorpe | All door-ways, |
| | | before going forward, |
| | | should be looked to; |
| | | for difficult it is to know |
| | | where foes may sit |
| | | within a dwelling. |

Bellows Verse 1

Within the gates
ere a man shall go,
(Full warily let him watch,)
Full long let him look about him;
For little he knows
where a foe may lurk,
And sit in the seats within.

Bray

At every door-way,
before one enters,
one should spy round,
one should pry round
for uncertain is the witting
that there be no foeman sitting,
within, before one on the floor

Verse 2 — Old Norse

Gefendr heilir!
Gestr er inn kominn,
hvar skal sitja sjá?
Mjök er bráðr
sá er á bröndum skal
síns of freista frama.

Thorpe

Givers, hail!
A guest is come in:
where shall he sit?
In much haste is he,
who on the ways
has to try his luck.

Hail to the giver! Bellows Verse
A guest has come; 2
Where shall the stranger sit?
Swift shall he be who,
with swords shall try
The proof of his might to make.

Hail, you givers! Bray
A guest is come;
say! Where shall he sit within?
Much pressed is he
who fain on the hearth
would seek for warmth and weal.

| Verse | Old | Elds er þörf |
|---|---|---|
| 3 | Norse | þeims inn er kominn |
| | | ok á kné kalinn. |
| | | Matar ok váða |
| | | er manni þörf, |
| | | þeim er hefr um fjall farit. |

Thorpe Fire is needful to him
who is come in,
and whose knees are frozen;
food and raiment a man requires,
wheo'er the fell has travelled.

Bellows Verse 3

Fire he needs
who with frozen knees
Has come from the cold without;
Food and clothes
must the farer have,
The man from the mountains
come.

Bray

He has need of fire,
who now is come,
numbed with cold to the knee;
food and clothing
the wanderer craves
who has fared over the rimy fell.

Verse 4 — Old Norse

Vatns er þörf<br>
þeim er til verðar kemr,<br>
þerru ok þjóðlaðar,<br>
góðs of æðis,<br>
ef sér geta mætti,<br>
orðs ok endrþögu.

Thorpe

Water to him is needful<br>
who for refection comes,<br>
a towel and hospitable invitation,<br>
a good reception;<br>
if he can get it,<br>
discourse and answer.

Bellows Verse 4

Water and towels
and welcoming speech
Should he find who comes,
to the feast;
If renown he would get,
and again be greeted,
Wisely and well must he act.

Bray

He craves for water,
who comes for refreshment,
drying and friendly bidding,
marks of good will,
fair fame if it is won,
and welcome once and again.

Verse 5

Old Norse

Vits er þörf
þeim er víða ratar;
dælt er heima hvat;
at augabragði verðr
sá er ekki kann
ok með snotrum sitr.

Thorpe

Wit is needful to him
who travels far:
at home all is easy.
A laughing-stock is he
who nothing knows,
and with the instructed sits.

Bellows Verse 5

Wits must he have
who wanders wide,
But all is easy at home;
At the witless man
the wise shall wink
When among such men he sits.

Bray

He has need of his wits
who wanders wide,
anything simple
will serve at home;
but a gazing-stock
is the fool who sits
mid the wise,
and nothing knows.

Verse 6

Old Norse

At hyggjandi sinni
skyli-t maðr hræsinn vera,
heldr gætinn at geði;
þá er horskr ok þögull
kemr heimisgarða til,
sjaldan verðr víti vörum,
þvíat óbrigðra vin
fær maðr aldregi
en mannvit mikit.

Thorpe

Of his understanding
no one should be proud,
but rather in conduct cautious.
When the prudent and taciturn
come to a dwelling,
harm seldom befalls the cautious;
for a firmer friend
no man ever gets
than great sagacity.

A man shall not boast | Bellows Verse 6
of his keenness of mind,
But keep it close in his breast;
To the silent and wise
does ill come seldom
When he goes as guest to a house;
(For a faster friend
one never finds
Than wisdom tried and true.)

Let no man glory | Bray
in the greatness of his mind,
but rather keep watch
over his wits.
Cautious and silent
let him enter a dwelling;
to the heedful
comes seldom harm,
for none can find
a more faithful friend
than the wealth of mother wit.

Verse 7

Old Norse

Inn vari gestr,
er til verðar kemr,
þunnu hljóði þegir,
eyrum hlýðir,
en augum skoðar;
svá nýsisk fróðra hverr fyrir.

Thorpe

A wary guest,
who to refection comes,
keeps a cautious silence,
with his ears listens,
and with his eyes observes:
so explores every prudent man.

Bellows Verse 7

The knowing guest
who goes to the feast,
In silent attention sits;
With his ears he hears,
with his eyes he watches,
Thus wary are wise men all.

Bray

Let the wary stranger
who seeks refreshment
keep silent
with sharpened hearing
with his ears let him listen,
and look with his eyes;
thus each wise man
spies out the way.

Verse 8

Old Norse

Hinn er sæll,
er sér of getr
lof ok líknstafi;
ódælla er við þat,
er maðr eiga skal
annars brjóstum í.

Thorpe

He is happy,
who for himself obtains
fame and kind words:
less sure is that
which a man must have
in another's breast.

Bellows Verse 8

Happy the one
who wins for himself
Favour and praises fair;
Less safe by far
is the wisdom found
That is hid in another's heart.

Bray

Happy is he who wins for himself
fair fame and kindly words;
but uneasy is that
which a man owns
while it lies in another's breast.

Verse 9

Old Norse

Sá er sæll,
er sjalfr of á
lof ok vit, meðan lifir;
þvíat ill ráð
hefr maðr oft þegit
annars brjóstum ór.

Thorpe

He is happy,
who in himself possesses
fame and wit while living;
for bad counsels
have oft been received
from another's breast.

Bellows Verse 9

Happy the man
who has while he lives
Wisdom and praise as well,
For evil counsel a man full oft
Has from another's heart.

Bray

Happy is he who has in himself
praise and wisdom in life;
for often does a man ill counsel get
when it is born in another's breast.

Verse 10

Old Norse

Byrði betri
berrat maðr brautu at
en sé manvit mikit
auði betra
þykkir þat í ókunnum stað
slíkt er válaðs vera

Thorpe

A better burden
no man bears on the way
than much good sense;
that is thought better than riches
in a strange place;
such is the recourse
of the indigent.

A better burden Bellows Verse
may no man bear 10
For wanderings wide
than wisdom;
It is better than wealth
on unknown ways,
And in grief a refuge it gives.

A better burden can no man bear Bray
on the way than his mother wit;
it is the refuge of the poor,
and richer it seems
than wealth in a world untried.

| Verse 11 | Old Norse | Byrði betri<br>berrat maðr brautu at<br>en sé manvit mikit<br>vegnest verra<br>vegra hann velli at<br>an sé ofdrykkja öls |
|---|---|---|
| | Thorpe | A worse provision on the way<br>he cannot carry<br>than too much beer-bibbing;<br>so good is not, as it is said,<br>beer for the sons of men. |

A better burden Bellows Verse 11
may no man bear
For wanderings wide
than wisdom;
Worse food for the journey
he brings not afield
Than an over-drinking of ale.

A better burden can no man bear Bray
on the way than his mother wit:
and no worse provision
can he carry with him
than too deep a draught of ale.

Verse 12 — Old Norse

Era svá gótt
sem gótt kveða
öl alda sonum
því at færa veit
er fleira drekkr
síns til geðs gumi

Thorpe

A worse provision
no man can take from table
than too much beer-bibbing:
for the more he drinks
the less control he has
of his own mind.

Bellows Verse 12

Less good there lies
than most believe
In ale for mortal men;
For the more he drinks
the less does man
Of his mind the mastery hold.

Bray

Less good than they say
for the sons of men
is the drinking often of ale:
for the more they drink,
the less can they think
and keep a watch over their wits.

| Verse 13 | Old Norse | Óminnishegri heitir<br>sá er yfir ölðrum þrumir<br>hann stelr geði guma<br>þess fugls fjöðrum<br>ek fjötraðr vask<br>í garði Gunnlaðar |
|---|---|---|
| | Thorpe | Oblivion's heron 'tis called that<br>over potations hovers;<br>he steals the minds of men.<br>With this bird's pinions<br>I was fettered<br>in Gunnlods dwelling. |

Over beer Bellows Verse
the bird of forgetfulness broods, 13
And steals the minds of men;
With the heron's feathers
fettered I lay
And in Gunnloth's house
was held.

A bird of unmindfulness Bray
Flutters over ale feasts,
wiling away men's wits:
with the feathers of that fowl
I was fettered once
in the garths of Gunnlos below.

| Verse 14 | Old Norse | Ölr ek varð<br>varð ofrölvi<br>at hins fróða Fjalars<br>því er ölðr bazt<br>at aptr of heimtir<br>hverr sitt geð gumi |
|---|---|---|
| | Thorpe | Drunk I was, I was over-drunk,<br>at that cunning Fialar's.<br>It's the best drunkenness,<br>when everyone after it<br>regains his reason. |

Bellows Verse 14

Drunk I was, I was dead-drunk,
When with Fjalar wise I was;
'Tis the best of drinking
if back one brings
His wisdom with him home.

Bray

Drunk was I then,
I was over drunk
in that crafty Jotun's court.
But best is an ale feast
when man is able
to call back his wits at once.

Verse 15 Old Norse

Þagalt ok hugalt
skyli þjóðans barn
ok vígdjarft vera
glaðr ok reifr
skyli gumna hverr
unz sínn bíðr bana

Thorpe

Taciturn and prudent,
and in war daring,
should a king's children be;
joyous and liberal
every one should be
until his hour of death.

The son of a king Bellows Verse
shall be silent and wise, 15
And bold in battle as well;
Bravely and gladly a man shall go,
Till the day of his death is come.

Silent and thoughtful Bray
and bold in strife
the prince's bairn should be.
Joyous and generous
let each man show him
till he shall suffer death.

| Verse 16 | Old Norse | Ósnjallr maðr<br>hyggsk munu ey lifa<br>ef hann við víg varask<br>en elli gefr<br>honum engi frið<br>þótt honum geirar gefi |
|---|---|---|
| | Thorpe | A cowardly man<br>thinks he will ever live,<br>if warfare he avoids;<br>but old age<br>will give him no peace,<br>though spears may spare him. |

The sluggard believes — Bellows Verse 16
he shall live forever,
If the fight he faces not;
But age shall not grant him
the gift of peace,
Though spears may spare his life.

A coward believes — Bray
he will ever live
if he keep him safe from strife:
but old age leaves him
not long in peace
though spears may spare his life.

| Verse 17 | Old Norse | Kópir afglapi<br>er til kynnis kømr<br>þylsk hann umbeða þrumir<br>alt er senn<br>ef hann sylg um getr<br>uppi er þá geð guma |
|---|---|---|
| | Thorpe | A fool gapes<br>when to a house he comes,<br>to himself mutters or is silent;<br>but all at once,<br>if he gets drink,<br>then is the man's mind displayed. |

The fool is agape Bellows Verse
when he comes to the feast, 17
He stammers or else is still;
But soon
if he gets a drink is it seen
What the mind of the man is like.

A fool will gape Bray
when he goes to a friend,
and mumble only, or mope;
but pass him the ale cup
and all in a moment
the mind of that man is shown.

| Verse 18 | Old Norse | Sá einn veit<br>er víða ratar<br>ok hefr fjölð um farit<br>hverju geði<br>stýrir gumna hverr<br>sá er vitandi er vits |
|---|---|---|
| | Thorpe | He alone knows<br>who wanders wide,<br>and has much experienced,<br>by what disposition<br>each man is ruled,<br>who common sense possesses. |

Bellows Verse 18

He alone is aware
who has wandered wide,
And far abroad has fared,
How great a mind
is guided by him
That wealth of wisdom has.

Bray

He knows alone
who has wandered wide,
and far has fared on the way,
what manner of mind
a man owns
who is wise of head and heart.

Verse 19 — Old Norse

Haldit maðr á keri
drekki þó at hófi mjöð
mæli þarft eða þegi
ókynnis þess
var þik engi maðr
at þú gangir snemma at sofa

Thorpe

Let a man hold the cup,
yet of the mead drink moderately,
speak sensibly or be silent.
As of a fault
no man will admonish thee,
if thou goest betimes to sleep.

Bellows Verse 19

Shun not the mead,
but drink in measure;
Speak to the point or be still;
For rudeness
none shall rightly blame thee
If soon thy bed thou seek.

Bray

Keep not the mead cup
but drink your measure;
speak needful words or none:
none shall upbraid you
for lack of breeding
if soon you seek'st your rest.

Verse 20

Old Norse

Gröðugr halr
nema geðs viti
etr sér aldrtrega
opt fær hlœgis
er með horskum kømr
manni heimskum magi

Thorpe

A greedy man,
if he be not moderate,
eats to his mortal sorrow.
Often his belly draws laughter
on a silly man,
who among the prudent comes.

Bellows Verse 20

The greedy man,
if his mind be vague,
Will eat till sick he is;
The vulgar man,
when among the wise,
To scorn by his belly is brought.

Bray

A greedy man,
if he be not mindful,
eats to his own life's hurt:
often the belly of the fool
will bring him to scorn
when he seeks
the circle of the wise.

Verse 21 — Old Norse

Hjarðir þat vitu
nær þær heim skulu
ok ganga þá af grasi
en ósviðr maðr
kann ævagi
síns um mál maga

Thorpe

Cattle know when to go home,
and then from grazing cease;
but a foolish man
never knows
his stomach's measure.

The herds know well — Bellows Verse 21
when home they shall fare,
And then from the grass they go;
But the foolish man
his belly's measure
Shall never know aright.

Herds know the hour — Bray
of their going home
and turn them again
from the grass;
but never is found a foolish man
who knows the measure
of his maw.

Verse 22 — Old Norse

Vesall maðr
ok illa skapi
hlær at hvívetna
hitki hann veit
er hann vita þyrpti
at hann era vamma vanr

Thorpe

A miserable man,
and ill-conditioned,
sneers at every thing:
one thing he knows not,
which he ought to know,
that he is not free from faults.

A paltry man and poor of mind Bellows Verse 22
At all things ever mocks;
For never he knows,
what he ought to know,
That he is not free from faults.

The miserable man Bray
and evil minded
makes of all things mockery,
and knows not
that which he best should know,
that he is not free from faults.

Verse 23

Old Norse

Ósviðr maðr
vakir um allar nætr
ok hyggr at hvívetna
þá er móðr
er at morni kømr
alt er vil sem var

Thorpe

A foolish man is all night awake,
pondering over everything;
he then grows tired;
and when morning comes,
all is lament as before.

The witless man Bellows Verse
is awake all night, 23
Thinking of many things;
Care-worn he is
when the morning comes,
And his woe is just as it was.

The unwise man Bray
is awake all night,
and ponders everything over;
when morning comes
he is weary in mind,
and all is a burden as ever.

Verse 24

Old Norse

Ósnotr maðr
hyggr sér alla vera
viðhlæjendr vini
hitki hann fiðr
þótt þeir um hann fár lesi
ef hann með snotrum sitr

Thorpe

A foolish man
thinks all who on him smile
to be his friends;
he feels it not,
although they speak ill of him,
when he sits among the clever.

Bellows Verse 24

The foolish man
for friends all those
Who laugh at him will hold;
When among the wise
he marks it not
Though hatred of him they speak.

Bray

The unwise man
weens all who smile
and flatter him are his friends,
nor notes how often
they speak him ill
when he sits
in the circle of the wise.

Verse 25

Old Norse

Ósnotr maðr
hyggr sér alla vera
viðhlæjendr vini
þá þat fiðr
er at þingi kømr
at hann á formælendr fá

Thorpe

A foolish man
thinks all who speak him fair
to be his friends;
but he will find,
if into court he comes,
that he has few advocates.

The foolish man — Bellows Verse 25
for friends all those
Who laugh at him will hold;
But the truth
when he comes
to the council he learns,
That few in his favour will speak.

The unwise man — Bray
weens all who smile
and flatter him are his friends;
but when he shall come into court
he shall find
there are few to defend his cause.

| Verse 26 | Old Norse | Ósnotr maðr<br>þykkisk alt vita<br>ef hann á sér í vá veru<br>hitki hann veit<br>hvat hann skal við kveða<br>ef hans freista firar |
|---|---|---|
| | Thorpe | A foolish man<br>thinks he knows everything<br>if placed in unexpected difficulty;<br>but he knows not what to answer,<br>if to the test he is put. |

Bellows Verse 26

An ignorant man
thinks that all he knows,
When he sits by himself
in a corner
But never what answer
to make he knows,
When others with questions
come.

Bray

The unwise man
thinks all to know
while he sits in a sheltered nook;
but he knows not one thing,
what he shall answer,
if men shall put him to proof.

Verse 27 Old Norse

Ósnotr maðr
er með 54re i kømr
þat er bazt at hann þegi
engi þat veit
at hann ekki kann
name hann mæli til mart
veita maðr
hinn er vætki veit
þótt hann mæli til mart

Thorpe

A foolish man,
who among people comes,
had best be silent;
for no one knows
that he knows nothing,
unless he talks too much.
He who knew nothing
will still know nothing,
talk he ever so much.

Bellows Verse 27

A witless man,
when he meets with men,
Had best in silence abide;
For no one shall find
that nothing he knows,
If his mouth is not open too much.
(But a man knows not,
if nothing he knows,
When his mouth
has been open too much.)

Bray

For the unwise man
it is best to be mute
when he come amid the crowd,
for none is aware of his lack of wit
if he wastes not too many words;
for he who lacks wit
shall never learn
though his words
flow never so fast.

Verse 28 Old Norse

Fróðr sá þykkisk
er fregna kann
ok segja hit sama
eyvitu leyna
megu ýta synir
því er gengr of guma

Thorpe

He thinks himself wise,
who can ask questions
and converse also;
conceal his ignorance no one can,
because it circulates among men.

Wise shall he seem  Bellows Verse 28
who well can question,
And also answer well;
Nought is concealed
that men may say
Among the sons of men.

Wise he is deemed  Bray
who can question well,
and also answer back:
the sons of men
can no secret make
of the tidings told in their midst.

Verse 29 Old Norse

Œrna mælir
sá er eva þegir
staðlausu stafi
hraðmælt tunga
nema haldendr eigi
opt sér ógótt um gelr

Thorpe

He utters too many futile words
who is never silent;
a garrulous tongue,
if it be not checked,
sings often to its own harm.

Often he speaks Bellows Verse
who never is still 29
With words that win no faith;
The babbling tongue,
if a bridle it find not,
Oft for itself sings ill.

Too many unstable words Bray
are spoken by him
who never holds his peace;
the hasty tongue
sings its own mishap
if it be not bridled in.

Verse 30

Old Norse

At augabragði
skala maðr anna hafa
þótt til kynnis komi
margr þá fróðr þykkisk
ef hann freginn erat
ok nái hann þurrfjallr þruma

Thorpe

For a gazing-stock
no man shall have another,
although he come a stranger
to his house.
Many a one thinks himself wise,
if he is not questioned,
and can sit in a dry habit.

In mockery Bellows Verse
no one a man shall hold, 30
Although he fare to the feast;
Wise seems one oft,
if nought he is asked,
And safely he sits dry-skinned.

Let no man be held Bray
as a laughing-stock,
though he is a guest for a meal
wise enough seem many
while they sit dry-skinned
and are not put to proof.

Verse Old Fróðr þykkisk
31 Norse sá er flótta tekr
gestr at gest hæðinn
veita görla
sá er of verði glissir
þótt hann með grömum glami

Thorpe Clever thinks himself the guest
who jeers a guest,
if he takes to flight.
Knows it not certainly
he who prates at meat,
whether he babbles among foes.

Bellows Verse 31

Wise a guest holds it
to take to his heels,
When mock of another he makes;
But little he knows
who laughs at the feast,
Though he mocks
in the midst of his foes.

Bray

A guest thinks him witty
who mocks at a guest
and runs from his wrath away;
but none can be sure
who jests at a meal
that he makes not fun among foes.

Verse 32 Old Norse

Gunnar margir
erusk gagnhollir
en at virði vrekask
aldar róg
þat mun æ vera
órir gestr við gest

Thorpe

Many men
are mutually well-disposed,
yet at table
will torment each other.
That strife will ever be;
guest will guest irritate.

Friendly of mind — Bellows Verse
are many men, 32
Till feasting they mock
at their friends;
To mankind a bane
must it ever be
When guests together strive.

Often, though their hearts — Bray
lean towards one another,
friends are divided at table;
ever the source of strife it will be,
that guest will anger guest.

Verse 33 Old Norse

Árliga verðar
skyli maðr opt fá
nema til kynnis komi
sitr ok snópir
lætr sem solginn sé
ok kann fregna at fá

Thorpe

Early meals
a man should often take,
unless to a friend's house he goes;
else he will sit and mope,
will seem half-famished,
and can of few things inquire.

Bellows Verse 33

Oft should one
make an early meal,
Nor fasting come to the feast;
Else he sits and chews
as if he would choke,
And little is able to ask.

Bray

A man should take
always his meals betimes
unless he visit a friend,
or he sits and mopes,
and half famished seems,
and can ask or answer nothing.

Verse 34 Old Norse

Afhvart mikit
er til ills vinar
þótt á brautu búi
en til góðs vinar
liggja gagnvegir
þótt hann sé firr farinn

Thorpe

Long is and indirect
the wayto a bad friend's,
though by the road he dwell;
but to a good friend's
the paths lie direct,
though he be far away.

Crooked and far
is the road to a foe,
Though his house
on the highway be;
But wide and straight
is the way to a friend,
Though far away he fare.

Bellows Verse 34

Long is the round
to a false friend leading,
even if he dwell on the way:
but though far off fared,
to a faithful friend
straight are the roads and short.

Bray

Verse 35 Old Norse

Ganga skal
skala gestr vera
ey í einum stað
ljúfr verðr leiðr
ef lengi sitr
annars fletjum á

Thorpe

A guest should depart,
not always stay in one place.
The welcome
becomes unwelcome,
if he too long continues
in another's house.

Bellows Verse 35

Forth shall one go,
nor stay as a guest
In a single spot forever;
Love becomes loathing
if long one sits
By the hearth in another's home.

Bray

A guest must depart
again on his way,
nor stay in the same place ever;
if he bide too long
on another's bench
the loved one soon becomes
loathed.

Verse 36 Old Norse

Bú er betra
þótt lítit sé
halr er heima hverr
þótt tvær geitr
eigi ok taugreptan sal
þat er þó betra an bœn

Thorpe

One's own house is best,
small though it be;
at home is every one
his own master.
Though he but two goats possess,
and a straw-thatched cot,
even that is better than begging.

Better a house, | Bellows Verse 36
though a hut it be,
A man is master at home;
A pair of goats
and a patched-up roof
Are better far than begging.

One's own house is best, | Bray
though small it may be;
each man is master at home;
though he have but two goats
and a bark-thatched hut
it is better than craving a boon.

Verse 37

Old Norse

Bú er betra
þótt lítit sé
halr er heima hverr
blóðugt er hjarta
þeims biðja skal
sér í mál hvert matar

Thorpe

One's own house is best,
small though it be,
at home is every one
his own master.
Bleeding at heart is he,
who has to ask for food
at every meal-tide.

Bellows Verse 37

Better a house, though a hut it be,
A man is master at home;
His heart is bleeding
who needs must beg
When food he fain would have.

Bray

One's own house is best,
though small it may be,
each man is master at home;
with a bleeding heart
will he beg, who must,
his meat at every meal.

| | | |
|---|---|---|
| Verse 38 | Old Norse | Vápnum sínum<br>skala maðr velli á<br>feti ganga framar<br>því at óvist er at vita<br>nær verðr á vegum úti<br>geirs um þörf guma |
| | Thorpe | Leaving in the field his arms,<br>let no man<br>go a foot's length forward;<br>for it is hard to know<br>when on the way<br>a man may need his weapon. |

Away from his arms — Bellows Verse 38
in the open field
A man should fare not a foot;
For never he knows
when the need for a spear
Shall arise on the distant road.

Let a man never stir — Bray
on his road a step
without his weapons of war;
for unsure is the knowing
when need shall arise
of a spear on the way without.

| Verse 39 | Old Norse | Fanca ec mildan mann<br>eþa sva matar goðan,<br>at ei vęri þiggia þegit,<br>eþa sins fiar<br>svá gjöflan<br>at leið sé laun ef þiggr |
|---|---|---|

Thorpe

I have never found a man
so bountiful, or so hospitable
that he refused a present;
or of his property so liberal
that he scorned a recompense.

If wealth a man Bellows Verse
has won for himself, 39
Let him never suffer in need;
Oft he saves for a foe
what he plans for a friend,
For much goes worse
than we wish.

Let no man stint him Bray
and suffer need
of the wealth he has won in life;
often is saved for a foe
what was meant for a friend,
and much goes worse
than one weens.

| Verse 40 | Old Norse | Féar síns<br>er fengit hefir<br>skylit maðr þörf þola<br>opt sparein leiðum<br>þats hefir ljúfum hugat<br>mart gengr verr en varir |
|---|---|---|
| | Thorpe | Of the property<br>which he has gained<br>no man should suffer need;<br>for the hated oft is spared<br>what for the dear was destined.<br>Much goes worse<br>than is expected. |

None so free with gifts Bellows Verse
or food have I found 40
That gladly he took not a gift,
Nor one who so widely
scattered his wealth
That of recompense
hatred he had.

Found none so noble Bray
or free with his food,
who was not gladdened
with a gift,
nor one who gave
of his gifts such store
but he loved reward,
could he win it.

Verse 41 Old Norse

Vápnum ok váðum
skulu vinir gleðjask
þat er á sjalfum sýnst
viðr gefendr ok endrgefendr
erusk vinir lengst,
ef þat bíðr at verða vel

Thorpe

With arms and vestments
friends should each other gladden,
those which are
in themselves most sightly.
Givers and requiters
are longest friends,
if all [else] goes well.

Friends shall gladden each other  Bellows Verse 41
with arms and garments,
As each for himself can see;
Gift-givers' friendships
are longest found,
If fair their fates may be.

With raiment and arms  Bray
shall friends gladden each other,
so has one proved oneself;
for friends last longest,
if fate be fair
who give and give again.

Verse 42 Old Norse

Vin sínum
skal maðr vinr vera
ok gjalda gjöf við gjöf
hlátr við hlátri
skyli hölðar taka
en lausung við lygi

Thorpe

To his friend
a man should be a friend,
and gifts with gifts requite.
Laughter with laughter
men should receive,
but leasing with lying.

To his friend Bellows Verse
a man a friend shall prove, 42
And gifts with gifts requite;
But men shall mocking
with mockery answer,
And fraud with falsehood meet.

To his friend Bray
a man should bear him as friend,
and gift for gift betow,
laughter for laughter
let him exchange,
but leasing pay for a lie.

Verse 43

Old Norse

Vin sínum
skal maðr vinr vera
þeim ok þess vinr
en óvinar síns
skyli engi maðr
vinar vinr vera

Thorpe

To his friend
a man should be a friend;
to him and to his friend;
but of his foe
no man shall
the friend's friend be.

To his friend a man | Bellows Verse
a friend shall prove to him | 43
and the friend of his friend;
But never a man
shall friendship make
With one of his foeman's friends.

To his friend | Bray
a man should bear him as friend,
to him and a friend of his;
but let him beware
that he be not the friend
of one who is friend to his foe.

Verse 44 Old Norse

Veiztu ef þú vin átt
þanns þú vel trúir
ok vill þú af honum gótt geta
geði skalt við þann
blanda ok gjöfum skipta
fara at finna opt

Thorpe

Know, if thou hast a friend
whom thou fully trustest,
and from whom
thou woulds't good derive,
thou shouldst blend
thy mind with his,
and gifts exchange,
and often go to see him.

Bellows Verse 44

If a friend thou hast
whom thou fully wilt trust,
And good from him wouldst get,
Thy thoughts with his mingle,
and gifts shalt thou make,
And fare to find him oft.

Bray

Have you got a friend
that you trust well,
from whom you crave good?
Share your mind with him,
gifts exchange with him,
fare to find him often.

Verse 45 — Old Norse

Ef þú át annan
þanns þú illa trúir
vildu af honum þó gótt geta
fagrt skalt við þann mæla
en flátt hyggja
ok gjalda lausung við lygi

Thorpe

If thou hast another,
whom thou little trustest,
yet wouldst good
from him derive,
thou shouldst speak him fair,
but think craftily,
and leasing pay with lying.

If another thou hast — Bellows Verse
whom thou hardly wilt trust, 45
Yet good from him wouldst get,
Thou shalt speak him fair,
but falsely think,
And fraud with falsehood requite.

But have you one — Bray
whom you trust ill
yet from whom you crave good?
You shall speak him fair,
but falsely think,
and leasing pay for a lie

Verse 46 Old Norse

Þat er enn of þann
er þú illa trúir
ok þér er grunr at hans geði
hlæja skaltu við þeim
ok um hug mæla
glík skulu gjöld gjöfum

Thorpe

But of him yet further,
whom thou little trustest,
and thou suspectest his affection;
before him thou shouldst laugh,
and contrary
to thy thoughts speak
requital should the gift resemble.

Bellows Verse 46

So is it with him
whom thou hardly wilt trust,
And whose mind
thou mayst not know;
Laugh with him mayst thou,
but speak not thy mind,
Like gifts to his shalt thou give.

Bray

Yet further of him
whom you trusted ill,
and whose mind
thou dost misdoubt;
though shall laugh with him
but withhold your thought,
for gift with like gift
should be paid.

Verse 47 — Old Norse

Ungr var ek forðum
fór ek einn saman
þá varð ek villr vega
auðigr þóttumk
er ek annan fann
maðr er manns gaman

Thorpe

I was once young,
I was journeying alone,
and lost my way;
rich I thought myself,
when I met another.
Man is the joy of man.

Young was I once, Bellows Verse
and wandered alone, 47
And nought of the road I knew;
Rich did I feel
when a comrade I found,
For man is man's delight.

Young was I once, Bray
I walked alone,
and bewildered
seemed in the way;
then I found me another
and rich I thought me,
for man is the joy of man.

Verse 48 — Old Norse

Mildir frœknir
menn bazt lifa
sjaldan sút ala
en ósnjallr maðr
uggir hotvetna
sýtir æ gløggr við gjöfum

Thorpe

Liberal and brave men live best,
they seldom cherish sorrow;
but a base-minded man
dreads everything;
the niggardly is uneasy
even at gifts.

Bellows Verse 48

The lives of the brave
and noble are best,
Sorrows they seldom feed;
But the coward
fear of all things feels,
And not gladly the niggard gives.

Bray

Most blest is he
who lives free and bold
and nurses never a grief,
for the fearful man
is dismayed by anything,
and the mean one
mourns over giving.

Verse 49

Old Norse

Váðir mínar
gaf ek velli at
tveim trémönnum
rekkar þat þóttusk
er þeir ript höfðu
neiss er nøkkviðr halr

Thorpe

My garments in a field
I gave away
to two wooden men:
heroes they seemed to be,
when they got cloaks:
exposed to insult is a naked man.

Bellows Verse 49

My garments once
in a field I gave
To a pair of carven poles;
Heroes they seemed
when clothes they had,
But the naked man is nought.

Bray

My garments once
I gave in the field
to two land-marks made as men;
heroes they seemed
when once they were clothed;
it is the naked who suffer shame!

Verse 50

Old Norse

Hrørnar þöll
sú er stendr þorpi á
hlýrat henni börkr né barr
svá er maðr
sá er mangi ann
hvat skal hann lengi lifa?

Thorpe

A tree withers
that on a hill-top stands;
protects it neither bark nor leaves:
such is the man
whom no one favours:
why should he live long?

On the hillside drear Bellows Verse
the fir-tree dies, 50
All bootless its needles and bark;
It is like a man
whom no one loves,-
Why should his life be long?

The pine tree wastes Bray
which is perched on the hill,
nor bark nor needles shelter it;
such is the man that no one loves;
what should he live longer for?

Verse 51 Old Norse

Eldi heitari
brinn með illum vinum
friðr fimm daga,
en þá sloknar
es hinn sétti kømr
ok versnar allr vinskapr

Thorpe

Hotter than fire
love for five days burns
between false friends;
but is quenched
when the sixth day comes,
and friendship is all impaired.

Hotter than fire Bellows Verse
between false friends 51
Does friendship five days burn;
When the sixth day comes
the fire cools,
And ended is all the love.

Fiercer than fire among ill friends Bray
for five days love will burn;
but anon it is quenched,
when the sixth day comes,
and all friendship soon is spoiled.

Verse 52

Old Norse

Mikit eitt
skala manni gefa
opt kaupir sér í lítlu lof
með hálfum hleifi
ok með höllu keri
fekk ek mér félaga

Thorpe

Something great
is not [always] to be given,
praise is often for a trifle bought.
With half a loaf and a tilted vessel
I got myself a comrade.

Bellows Verse 52

No great thing
needs a man to give,
Oft little will purchase praise;
With half a loaf
and a half-filled cup
A friend full fast I made.

Bray

Not great things alone
must one give to another,
praise often is earned for nothing;
with half a loaf and a tilted bowl
I have found me many a friend.

Verse 53

Old Norse

Lítilla sanda
lítilla sæva
lítil eru geð guma
því at allir menn
urðut jafnspakir
hálf er öld hvar

Thorpe

Little are the sand-grains,
little the wits,
little the minds of [some] men;
for all men are not wise alike:
men are everywhere by halves.

Bellows Verse 53

A little sand has a little sea,
And small are the minds of men;
Though all men
are not equal in wisdom,
Yet half-wise only are all.

Bray

Little the sand if little the seas,
little are minds of men,
for never in the world
were all equally wise,
it is shared by the fools
and the sage.

Verse 54

Old Norse

Meðalsnotr
skyli manna hverr
æva til snotre i sé
þeim er fyrða
fegrst at lifa
er vel mart vitut

Thorpe

Moderately wise
should each one be,
but never over-wise:
of those men the lives are fairest,
who know much well.

Bellows Verse 54

A measure of wisdom
each man shall have,
But never too much
let him know;
The fairest lives do those men live
Whose wisdom wide has grown.

Bray

Wise in measure let each man be;
but let him not wax too wise;
for never the happiest
of men, is he who knows
much of many things.

Verse 55 — Old Norse

Meðalsnotr
skyli manna hverr
æva til snotr sé
því at snotrs manns hjarta
verðr sjaldan glatt,
ef sá er alsnotr er á

Thorpe

Moderately wise
should each one be,
but never over-wise;
for a wise man's heart
is seldom glad,
if he is all-wise who owns it.

A measure of wisdom — Bellows Verse 55
each man shall have,
But never too much
let him know;
For the wise man's heart
is seldom happy,
If wisdom too great he has won.

Wise in measure — Bray
should each man be;
but let him not wax too wise;
seldom a heart will sing with joy
if the owner be all too wise.

Verse 56 | Old Norse

Meðalsnotr
skyli manna hverr
æva til snotr sé
ørlög sín
viti engi fyrir
þeim er sorgalausastr sefi

Thorpe

Moderately wise
should each one be,
but never over-wise.
His destiny let know
no man beforehand;
his mind will be freest from' care.

A measure of wisdom — Bellows Verse 56
each man shall have,
But never too much
let him know;
Let no man the fate
before him see,
For so is he freest from sorrow.

Wise in measure — Bray
should each man be,
but never let him wax too wise:
who does not look forward
to learn his fate
unburdened heart will bear.

Verse 57 — Old Norse

Brandr af brandi
brinn unz brunninn er
funi kveykisk af funa
maðr af manni
verðr at máli kuðr
en til dœlskr af dul

Thorpe

Brand burns from brand
until it is burnt out;
fire is from fire quickened.
Man to man
becomes known by speech,
but a fool by his bashful silence.

A brand from a brand
is kindled and burned,
And fire from fire begotten;
And man by his speech
is known to men,
And the stupid by their stillness.

Bellows Verse 57

Brand kindles from brand
till it be burned,
spark is kindled from spark,
man unfold him
by speech with man,
but grows over secret
through silence.

Bray

Verse 58

Old Norse

Ár skal rísa
sá er annars vill
fé eða fjör hafa
sjaldan liggjandi úlfr
lær um getr
né sofandi maðr sigr

Thorpe

He should early rise,
who another's property
or life desires to have.
Seldom a sluggish wolf gets prey,
or a sleeping man victory.

He must early go forth
who fain the blood
Or the goods of another
would get;
The wolf that lies idle
shall win little meat,
Or the sleeping man success.

Bellows Verse 58

He must rise betimes
who fain of another
or life or wealth would win;
scarce falls the prey
to sleeping wolves,
or to slumberers victory in strife.

Bray

Verse 59

Old Norse

Ár skal rísa
sá er á yrkendr fá
ok ganga síns verka á vit
mart um dvelr
þann er um morgin sefr
hálfr er auðr und hvötum

Thorpe

Early should rise he
who has few workers,
and go his work to see to;
greatly is he retarded
who sleeps the morn away.
Wealth half depends on energy.

Bellows Verse 59

He must early go forth
whose workers are few,
Himself his work to seek;
Much remains undone
for the morning-sleeper,
For the swift is wealth half won.

Bray

He must rise betimes
who has few to serve him,
and see to his work himself;
who sleeps at morning
is hindered much,
to the keen is wealth half-won.

Verse 60

Old Norse

Þurra skíða
ok þakinna næfra
þess kann maðr mjöt
ok þess viðar
er vinnask megi
mál ok misseri

Thorpe

Of dry planks and roof-shingles
a man knows the measure;
of the fire-wood that may suffice,
both measure and time.

Of seasoned shingles Bellows Verse
and strips of bark for the thatch 60
let one know his need,
And how much of wood
he must have for a month,
Or in half a year he will use.

Of dry logs saved Bray
and roof-bark stored
a man can know the measure,
of fire-wood too
which should last him out
quarter and half years to come.

Verse 61 — Old Norse

Þveginn ok mettr
ríði maðr þingi at
þótt hann sét væddr til vel
skúa ok bróka
skammisk engi maðr
né hests in heldr
þótt hann hafit góðan

Thorpe

Washed and refected
let a man ride to the Thing,
although his garments
be not too good;
of his shoes and breeches
let no one be ashamed,
nor of his horse,
although he have not a good one.

Washed and fed
to the council fare,
But care not too much
for thy clothes;
Let none be ashamed
of his shoes and hose,
Less still of the steed he rides,
(Though poor
be the horse he has.)

Bellows Verse 61

Fed and washed
should one ride to court
though in garments
none too new;
you shall not shame you
for shoes or breeks,
nor yet for a sorry steed.

Bray

Verse 62

Old Norse

Snapir ok gnapir
er til sævar kømr
örn á aldinn mar
svá er maðr
er með mörgum kømr
ok á formælendr fá

Thorpe

Inquire and impart
should every man of sense,
who will be accounted sage.
Let one only know,
a second may not;
if three, all the world knows.

To question and answer | Bellows Verse
must all be ready | 62
Who wish to be known as wise;
Tell one thy thoughts,
but beware of two,--
All know what is known to three.

Each man who is wise | Bray
and would wise be called
must ask and answer aright.
Let one know your secret,
but never a second, -
if three a thousand shall know.

Verse 63

Old Norse

Fregna ok segja
skal fróðra hverr
sá er vill heitinn horskr
einn vita
né annarr skal
þjóð veit ef þrír ro

Thorpe

Gasps and gapes,
when to the sea he comes,
the eagle over old ocean;
so is a man,
who among many comes,
and has few advocates.

When the eagle comes Bellows Verse
to the ancient sea, 63
He snaps and hangs his head;
So is a man
in the midst of a throng
Who few to speak for him finds.

As the eagle who comes Bray
to the ocean shore,
Sniffs and hangs her head,
Dumfounded is he
who finds at the Thing
No supporters to plead his case.

Verse 64 Old Norse

Ríki sitt
skyli ráðsnotra
hverr í hófi hafa
þá hann þat finnr
er með frœknum kømr
at engi er einna hvatastr

Thorpe

His power
should every sagacious man
use with discretion;
for he will find,
when among the bold he comes,
that no one alone is doughtiest.

Bellows Verse 64

The man who is prudent
a measured use
Of the might he has will make;
He finds when among
the brave he fares
That the boldest he may not be.

Bray

A wise counselled man
will be mild in bearing
and use his might in measure,
lest when he come
his fierce foes among
he find others fiercer than he.

Verse 65 Old Norse

Orða þeira
er maðr öðrum segir
opt hann gjöld um getr

Thorpe

*Circumspect and reserved**
*every man should be,*
*and wary in trusting friends.*
Of the words that a man
says to another
he often pays the penalty.

* *The first three lines are a later interpolation*

Bellows Verse
65

Oft for the words
that to others one speaks
He will get but an evil gift.

*Each man should be watcfhful*
*and wary in speech,*
*and slow to put faith in a friend.*
For the words
which one to another speaks
he may wind reward of ill.

Bray

** The first three lines are a later interpolation*

Verse 66

Old Norse

Mikilsti snemma
kom ek í marga staði
en til síð í suma
öl var drukkit
sumt var ólagat
sjaldan hittir leiðr í lið

Thorpe

Much too early
I came to many places,
but too late to others:
the beer was drunk,
or not ready:
the disliked
seldom hits the moment.

Too early  Bellows Verse 66
to many a meeting I came,
And some too late have I sought;
The beer was all drunk,
or not yet brewed;
Little the loathed man finds.

At many a feast I was far too late,  Bray
and much too soon at some;
drunk was the ale
or yet unserved:
never hits he the joint
who is hated.

Verse 67

Old Norse

Hér ok hvar
myndi mér heim of boðit
ef þyrftak at málungi mat
eða tvau lær hengi
at ins tryggva vinar
þars ek hafða eitt etit

Thorpe

Here and there
I should have been invited,
if I a meal had needed;
or two hams had hung,
at that true friend's,
where of one I had eaten.

Bellows Verse 67

To their homes
men would bid me
hither and yon,
If at meal-time I needed no meat,
Or would hang two hams
in my true friend's house,
Where only one I had eaten.

Bray

Here and there to a home
I had haply been asked
had I needed no meat
at my meals,
or were two hams left hanging
in the house of that friend
where I had partaken of one.

Verse Old Eldr er beztr
68 Norse með ýta sonum
ok sólar sýn
heilyndi sitt
ef maðr hafa náir
án við löst at lifa

Thorpe Fire is best
among the sons of men,
and the sight of the sun,
if his health a man can have,
with a life free from vice.

Bellows Verse 68

Fire for men is the fairest gift,
And power to see the sun;
Health as well,
if a man may have it,
And a life not stained with sin.

Bray

Most dear is fire
to the sons of men,
most sweet the sight of the sun;
good is health
if one can but keep it,
and to live a life without shame.

Verse 69 — Old Norse

Erat maðr alls vesall
þótt hann sé illa heill
sumr er af sonum sæll
sumr af frændum
sumr af fé œrnu
sumr af verkum vel.

Thorpe

No man lacks everything,
although his health be bad:
one in his sons is happy,
one in his kin,
one in abundant wealth,
one in his good works.

Bellows Verse 69

All wretched is no man,
though never so sick;
Some from their sons have joy,
Some win it from kinsmen,
and some from their wealth,
And some from worthy works.

Bray

Not reft of all is he who is ill,
for some are blest in their bairns,
some in their kin
and some in their wealth,
and some in working well.

Verse 70

Old Norse

Betra er lifðum
en sé ólifðum
ey getr kvikr kú
eld sá ek upp brenna
auðgum manni fyrir
en úti var dauðr fyr durum

Thorpe

It is better to live,
even to live miserably;
a living man
can always get a cow.
I saw fire consume
the rich man's property,
and death stood without his door.

It is better to live Bellows Verse
than to lie a corpse, 70
The live man catches the cow;
I saw flames rise
for the rich man's pyre,
And before his door he lay dead.

More blest are the living Bray
than the lifeless,
it is the living
who come by the cow;
I saw the hearth-fire burn
in the rich man's hall
and himself
lying dead at the door.

Verse 71 Old Norse

Haltr ríðr hrossi
hjörð rekr handarvanr
daufr vegr ok dugir
blindr er betri
en brenndr sé
nýtr manngi nás

Thorpe

The halt can ride on horseback,
the one-handed drive cattle;
the deaf fight and be useful:
to be blind is better
than to be burnt
no one gets good from a corpse.

The lame rides a horse, Bellows Verse
the handless is herdsman, 71
The deaf in battle is bold;
The blind man is better
than one that is burned,
No good can come of a corpse.

The lame can ride rose, Bray
the handless drive cattle,
the deaf one can fight and prevail,
it is happier for the blind
than for him on the bale-fire,
but no man has care for a corpse.

Verse 72

Old Norse

Sonr er betri
þótt sé síð of alinn
eptir genginn guma
sjaldan bautarsteinar
standa brautu nær
nema reisi niðr at nið

Thorpe

A son is better,
even if born late,
after his father's departure.
Gravestones seldom
stand by the way-side
unless raised
by a kinsman to a kinsman.

| | |
|---|---|
| A son is better,<br>though late he be born,<br>And his father<br>to death have fared;<br>Memory-stones seldom<br>stand by the road<br>Save when kinsman<br>honors his kin. | Bellows Verse<br>72 |

| | |
|---|---|
| Best have a son<br>though he be late born<br>and before him the father be dead:<br>seldom are stones<br>raised on the wayside<br>save by kinsmen to kinsmen. | Bray |

Verse 73 | Old Norse

Tveir 146re inn herjar
tunga er höfuðs bani
er mér í heðin hvern
handar væni

Thorpe

Two are adversaries:
the tongue is the bane of the head:
under every cloak
I expect a hand.

Two make a battle, Bellows Verse 73
the tongue slays the head;
In each furry coat
a fist I look for.

Two are hosts against one, Bray
the tongue is the head's bane,
'neath a rough hide
a hand may be hid.

Verse 74

Old Norse

Nótt verðr feginn<br>
sá er nesti trúir<br>
skammar ro skips rár<br>
hverf er haustgríma<br>
fjölð um viðrir<br>
á fimm dögum<br>
en meira á mánuði

Thorpe

At night is joyful he<br>
who is sure<br>
of travelling entertainment.<br>
[A ship's yards are short.]<br>
Variable is an autumn night.<br>
Many are the weather's changes<br>
in five days,<br>
but more in a month.

He welcomes the night — Bellows Verse
whose fare is enough, 74
(Short are the yards of a ship,)
Uneasy are autumn nights;
Full oft does the weather
change in a week,
And more in a month's time.

He is glad at night fall — Bray
who knows of his lodging,
short is the ship's berth,
and changeful the autumn night,
much veers the wind
before the fifth day
and blows round
yet more in a month.

Verse 75

Old Norse

Veita hinn
er vættki veit
margr verðr af aurum api
maðr er auðigr
annarr óauðigr
skylit þann vítka vár

Thorpe

He [only] knows not
who knows nothing,
that many a one apes another.
One man is rich, another poor:
let him not be thought
blameworthy.

A man knows not, Bellows Verse
if nothing he knows, 75
That gold oft apes begets;
One man is wealthy
and one is poor,
Yet scorn for him
none should know.

He who learns nothing Bray
will never know
how one is the fool of another,
for if one be rich another is poor
and for that should bear no blame.

| Verse 76 | Old Norse | Deyr fé<br>deyja frændr<br>deyr sjálfr it sama<br>en orðstírr<br>deyr aldregi<br>hveim er sér góðan getr |
|---|---|---|
| | Thorpe | Cattle die, kindred die,<br>we ourselves also die;<br>but the fair fame never dies<br>of him who has earned it. |

Cattle die, and kinsmen die, Bellows Verse 76
And so one dies one's self;
But a noble name will never die,
If good renown one gets.

Cattle die and kinsmen die, Bray
yourself too soon must die,
but one thing
will never die, I think
– the doom on each one dead.

Verse 77 Old Norse

Deyr fé
deyja frændr
deyr sjálfr it sama
ek veit einn
at aldri deyr
dómr um dauðan hvern

Thorpe

Cattle die, kindred die,
We ourselves also die;
But I know one thing
that never dies,
--judgment on each one dead.

Cattle die, and kinsmen die, Bellows Verse 77
And so one dies one's self;
One thing now that never dies,
The fame of a dead man's deeds.

Cattle die and kinsmen die, Bray
yourself too soon must die,
but one thing never,
I think, will die, -
fair fame of one who has earned.

Verse 78

Old Norse

Fullar grindr
sá ek fyr Fitjungs sonum
nú bera þeir vánarvöl
svá er auðr
sem augabragð
hann er valtastr vina

Thorpe

Full storehouses
I saw at Dives' sons':
now bear they the beggar's staff.
Such are riches;
as is the twinkling of an eye:
Of friends they are most fickle.

Among Fitjung's sons Bellows Verse 78
saw I well-stocked folds,--
Now bear they the beggar's staff;
Wealth is as swift
as a winking eye,
Of friends the falsest it is.

Full-stocked folds Bray
had the Fatling's sons,
who bear now a beggar's staff:
brief is wealth,
as the winking of an eye,
most faithless ever of friends.

Verse 79 Old Norse

Ósnotr maðr
ef eignask getr
fé eða fljóðs munuð
metnaðr honum þróask
en mannvit aldregi
fram gengr hann drjúgt í dul

Thorpe

A foolish man,
if he acquires wealth
or woman's love,
pride grows within him,
but wisdom never:
he goes on more
and more arrogant.

An unwise man, Bellows Verse
if a maiden's love 79
Or wealth he chances to win,
His pride will wax,
but his wisdom never,
Straight forward
he fares in conceit.

If haply a fool Bray
should find for himself
wealth or a woman's love,
pride waxes in him
but wisdom never
and onward he fares in his folly.

Verse 80

Old Norse

Þat er þá reynt
er þú at rúnum spyrr
inum reginkunnum
þeim er gerðu ginnregin
ok fáði fimbulþulr
þá hefir hann bazt ef hann þegir

Thorpe

Then 'tis made manifest,
if of runes thou questionest him,
those to the high ones known,
which the great powers invented,
and the great talker painted,
that he had best hold silence.

Certain is that Bellows Verse
which is sought from runes, 80
That the gods so great have made,
And the Master-Poet painted;
Certain is that
which is sought from runes,
The runes of the race of gods:
Silence is safest and best.

All will prove true Bray
that you ask of runes –
those that are come from the gods,
which the high Powers wrought,
and which Odin painted:
then silence is surely best.

Verse 81 Old Norse

At kveldi skal dag leyfa
konu er brennd er
mæki er reyndr er
mey er gefin er
ís er yfir kømr
öl er drukkit er

Thorpe

At eve the day is to be praised,
a woman after she is burnt,
a sword after it is proved,
a maid after she is married,
ice after it has passed away,
beer after it is drunk.

Give praise to the day at evening, Bellows Verse
to a woman on her pyre, 81
To a weapon which is tried,
to a maid at wed lock,
To ice when it is crossed,
to ale that is drunk.

Praise day at even, Bray
a wife when dead,
a weapon when tried,
a maid when married,
ice when it is crossed,
and ale when it is drunk.

Verse 82 Old Norse

Í vindi skal við höggva
veðri á sjó róa
myrkri við man spjalla
mörg eru dags augu
á skip skal skriðar orka
en á skjöld til hlífar
mæki höggs
en mey til kossa

Thorpe

In the wind one should
hew wood
in a breeze row out to sea,
in the dark talk with a lass:
many are the eyes of day.
In a ship voyages are to be made,
but a shield is for protection,
a sword for striking,
but a damsel for a kiss.

When the gale blows hew wood, Bellows Verse
in fair winds seek the water; 82
Sport with maidens at dusk,
for day's eyes are many;
From the ship seek swiftness,
from the shield protection,
Cuts from the sword,
from the maiden kisses.

Hew wood in wind, Bray
sail the seas in a breeze,
woo a maid in the dark,
- for day's eyes are many, -
work a ship for its gliding,
a shield for its shelter,
a sword for its striking,
a maid for her kiss;

Verse 83 Old Norse

Við eld skal öl drekka
en á ísi skríða
magran mar kaupa
en mæki saurgan
heima hest feita
en hund á búi

Thorpe

By the fire one should drink beer,
on the ice slide;
buy a horse that is lean,
a sword that is rusty;
feed a horse at home,
but a dog at the farm.

By the fire drink ale, Bellows Verse
over ice go on skates; 83
Buy a steed that is lean,
and a sword when tarnished,
The horse at home fatten,
the hound in thy dwelling.

Drink ale by the fire, Bray
but slide on the ice;
buy a steed when it is lanky,
a sword when it is rusty;
feed your horse neath a roof,
and your hound in the yard.

Verse 84 Old Norse

Meyjar orðum
skyli manngi trúa
né því er kveðr kona
því at á hverfanda hvéli
váru þeim hjörtu sköpuð
brigð í brjóst um lagit

Thorpe

In a maiden's words
no one should place faith,
nor in what a woman says;
for on a turning wheel
have their hearts been formed,
and guile
in their breasts been laid;

A man shall trust
not the oath of a maid,
Nor the word a woman speaks;
For their hearts
on a whirling wheel
were fashioned,
And fickle their breasts
were formed.

Bellows Verse 84

The speech of a maiden
should no man trust
nor the words
which a woman says;
for their hearts were shaped
on a whirling wheel
and falsehood
fixed in their breasts.

Bray

Verse 85

Old Norse

Brestanda boga
brennanda loga
gínanda úlfi
galandi kráku
rýtanda svíni
rótlausum viði
vaxanda vági
vellanda katli

Thorpe

In a creaking bow,
a burning flame,
a yawning wolf,
a chattering crow,
a grunting swine,
a rootless tree,
a waxing wave,
a boiling kettle,

In a breaking bow Bellows Verse
or a burning flame, 85
A ravening wolf
or a croaking raven,
In a grunting boar,
a tree with roots broken,
In billowy seas
or a bubbling kettle,

Breaking bow, Bray
or flaring flame,
ravening wolf,
or croaking raven,
routing swine,
or rootless tree,
waxing wave,
or seething cauldron,

Verse 86 Old Norse

Fljúganda fleini
fallandi báru
ísi einnættum
ormi hringlegnum
brúðar beðmálum
eða brotnu sverði
bjarnar leiki
eða barni konungs

Thorpe

A flying dart,
a falling billow,
a one night's ice,
a coiled serpent,
a woman's bed-talk,
or a broken sword,
a bear's play,
or a royal child,

Bellows Verse 86

In a flying arrow
or falling waters,
In ice new formed
or the serpent's folds,
In a bride's bed-speech
or a broken sword,
In the sport of bears
or in sons of kings,

Bray

flying arrows,
or falling billow,
ice of a night time,
coiling adder,
woman's bed-talk,
or broken blade,
play of bears
or a prince's child,

Verse 87 Old Norse

Sjúkum kálfi
sjálfráða þræli
völu vilmæli
val nýfeldum

Thorpe

A sick calf,
a self-willed thrall,
a flattering prophetess,
a corpse newly slain,
[a serene sky, a laughing lord,
a barking dog, and a harlot's grief];

In a calf that is sick — Bellows Verse 87
or a stubborn thrall,
A flattering witch
or a foe new slain.
"In a light, clear sky
or a laughing throng,
In the bowl of a dog
or a harlot's grief!"

sickly calf — Bray
or self-willed thrall,
witch's flattery,
new-slain foe,

Verse 88 Old Norse

Akri ársánum
trúi engi maðr
né til snemma syni
veðr ræðr akri
en vit syni
hætt er þeira hvárt

Thorpe

An early sown field
let no one trust,
nor prematurely in a son:
weather rules the field,
and wit the son,
each of which is doubtful;

Hope not too surely Bellows Verse
for early harvest, 88
Nor trust too soon in thy son;
The field needs good weather,
the son needs wisdom,
And oft is either denied.

Let none put faith Bray
in the first sown fruit
nor yet in his son too soon;
whim rules the child,
and weather the field,
each is open to chance.

Verse 89 Old Norse

Bróðurbana sínum
þótt á brautu mœti
húsi hálfbrunnu
hesti alskjótum
þá er jór ónýtr
ef einn fótr brotnar
verðit maðr svá tryggr
at þessu trúi öllu

Thorpe

A brother's murderer,
though on the high road met,
a half-burnt house,
an over-swift horse,
(a horse is useless,
if a leg be broken),
no man is so confiding
as to trust any of these.

Bellows Verse 89

In a brother's slayer,
if thou meet him abroad,
In a half-burned house,
in a horse full swift–
One leg is hurt
and the horse is useless–
None had ever such faith
as to trust in them all.

Bray

Brother's slayer,
though seen on the highway,
half burned house,
or horse too swift –
be never so trustful
as these to trust.

Verse 90

Old Norse

Svá er friðr kvenna
þeira er flátt hyggja
sem aki jó óbryddum
á ísi hálum
teitum tvévetrum
ok sé tamr illa
eða í byr óðum
beiti stjórnlausu
eða skyli haltr henda
hrein í þáfjalli

Thorpe

Such is the love of women,
who falsehood meditate,
as if one drove not rough-shod,
on slippery ice,
a spirited two-years old
and unbroken horse;
or as in a raging storm
a helmless ship is beaten;
or as if the halt were set to catch
a reindeer in the thawing fell.

The love of women fickle of will Bellows Verse
Is like starting o'er ice 90
with a steed unshod,
A two-year-old restive
and little tamed,
Or steering a rudderless ship
in a storm,
Or, lame, hunting reindeer
on slippery rocks.

Like the love of women Bray
whose thoughts are lies
is the driving un-roughshod
over slippery ice
of a two year old,
ill-tamed and gay;
or in a wild wind steering
a helmless ship,
or the lame catching reindeer
in the rime-thawed fell.

Verse 91

Old Norse

Bert ek nú mæli
því at ek bæði veit
brigðr er karla hugr konum
þá vér fegrst mælum
er vér flást hyggjum
þat tælir horska hugi

Thorpe

Openly I now speak,
because I both sexes know:
unstable are men's minds
towards women;
'tis then we speak most fair
when we most falsely think:
that deceives even the cautious.

Clear now will I speak, Bellows Verse 91
for I know them both,
Men false to women are found;
When fairest we speak,
then falsest we think,
Against wisdom
we work with deceit.

Now plainly I speak, Bray
since both I have seen;
unfaithful is man to maid;
we speak them fairest
when thoughts are falsest
and wile the wisest of hearts.

Verse 92 Old Norse

Fagrt skal mæla
ok fé bjóða
sá er vill fljóðs ást fá
líki leyfa
ins ljósa mans
sá fær er fríar

Thorpe

Fair shall speak,
and money offer,
who would obtain
a woman's love.
Praise the form of a fair damsel;
he gets who courts her.

Bellows Verse 92

Soft words shall he speak
and wealth shall he offer
Who longs for a maiden's love,
And the beauty praise
of the maiden bright;
He wins whose wooing is best.

Bray

Let him speak soft words
and offer wealth
who longs for a woman's love,
praise the shape
of the shining maid –
he wins who thus woos.

Verse 93 Old Norse

Ástar firna
skyli engi maðr
annan aldregi
opt fá á horskan
er á heimskan ne fá
lostfagrir litir

Thorpe

At love should no one
ever wonder in another:
a beauteous countenance
oft captivates the wise,
which captivates not the foolish.

Fault for loving let no man find Bellows Verse
Ever with any other; 93
Oft the wise are fettered,
where fools go free,
By beauty that breeds desire.

Never a whit Bray
should one blame another
whom love
has brought into bonds:
often a witching form
will fetch the wise
which does not hold
the heart of fools.

Verse 94 — Old Norse

Eyvitar firna
er maðr annan skal
þess er um margan gengr guma
heimska ór horskum
gørir hölða sonu
sá inn mátki munr

Thorpe

Let no one wonder
at another's folly,
it is the lot of many.
All-powerful desire
makes of the sons of men
fools even of the wise.

Bellows Verse 94

Fault with another
let no man find
For what touches many a man;
Wise men oft into witless fools
Are made by mighty love.

Bray

Never a whit
should one blame another
for a folly which many befalls;
the might of love
makes sons of men into fools
who once were wise.

Verse 95 Old Norse

Hugr einn þat veit
er býr hjarta nær
einn er hann sér um sefa
øng er sótt verri
hveim snotrum manni
en sér øngu at una

Thorpe

The mind only knows
what lies near the heart,
that alone is conscious
of our affections.
No disease is worse
to a sensible man
than not to be content
with himself.

Bellows Verse 95

The head alone knows
what dwells near the heart,
A man knows his mind alone;
No sickness is worse
to one who is wise
Than to lack the longed-for joy.

Bray

The mind knows alone
what is nearest the heart
and sees where the soul is turned:
no sickness seems to the wise so
sore
as in nothing to know content.

Verse 96 | Old Norse

Þat ek þá reynda
er ek í reyri sat
ok vættak míns munar
hold ok hjarta
var mér in horska mær
þeygi ek hana at heldr hefik

Thorpe

That I experienced,
when in the reeds I sat,
awaiting my delight.
Body and soul to me
was that discreet maiden:
nevertheless I possess her not.

Bellows Verse 96

This found I myself,
when I sat in the reeds,
And long my love awaited;
As my life
the maiden wise I loved,
Yet her I never had.

Bray

This once I felt when I sat
Without in the reeds,
and looked for my love;
body and soul of me
was that sweet maiden
yet never I won her as wife.

Verse Old Billings mey
97 Norse ek fann beðjum á
sólhvíta sofa
jarls ynði
þótti mér ekki vera
nema við þat lík at lifa

Thorpe Billing's lass
on her couch I found,
sun-bright, sleeping.
A prince's joy to me
seemed naught,
if not with that form to live.

Billing's daughter Bellows Verse 97
I found on her bed,
In slumber bright as the sun;
Empty appeared an earl's estate
Without that form so fair.

Billing's daughter Bray
I found on her bed,
fairer than sunlight sleeping,
and the sweets of lordship
seemed to me nothing,
save I lived with that lovely form.

Verse 98 Old Norse

Auk nær apni
skaltu Óðinn koma
ef þú vilt þér mæla man
alt eru ósköp
nema einir viti
slíkan löst saman

Thorpe

"Yet nearer eve
must thou, Óðinn, come,
if thou wilt talk the maiden over;
all will be disastrous,
unless we alone
are privy to such misdeed."

| | |
|---|---|
| "Óðinn, again at evening come,<br>If a woman thou wouldst win;<br>Evil it were if others than we<br>Should know of such a sin." | Bellows Verse<br>98 |

| | |
|---|---|
| "Yet nearer evening<br>come you, Óðinn,<br>if you will woo a maiden:<br>all were undone<br>save two knew alone<br>such a secret deed of shame." | Bray |

Verse 99 Old Norse

Aptr ek hvarf
ok unna þóttumk
vísum vilja frá
hitt ek hugða
at ek hafa mynda
geð hennar alt ok gaman

Thorpe

I returned,
thinking to love,
at her wise desire.
I thought I should obtain
her whole heart and love.

Away I hastened, Bellows Verse 99
hoping for joy,
And careless of counsel wise;
Well I believed
that soon I should win
Measureless joy with the maid.

So away I turned Bray
from my wise intent,
and deemed my joy assured,
for all her liking and all her love
I thought that I yet should win.

Verse 100

Old Norse

Svá kom ek næst
at in nýta var
vígdrótt öll um vakin
með brennandum ljósum
ok bornum viði
svá var mér vílstígr of vitaðr

Thorpe

When next I came
the bold warriors were all awake,
with lights burning,
and bearing torches:
thus was the way
to pleasure closed.

So came I next Bellows Verse
when night it was, 100
The warriors all were awake;
With burning lights
and waving brands
I learned my luckess way.

When I came before long Bray
the war troop bold
were watching and waking all:
with burning brands
and torches borne
they showed me
my sorrowful way.

| Verse 101 | Old Norse | Ok nær morni<br>er ek var enn um kominn<br>þá var saldrótt um sofin<br>grey eitt ek þá fann<br>innar góðu konu<br>bundit beðjum á |
|---|---|---|
| | Thorpe | But at the approach of morn,<br>when again I came,<br>the household all was sleeping;<br>the good damsel's dog alone<br>I found tied to the bed. |

At morning then, | Bellows Verse 101
when once more I came,
And all were sleeping still,
A dog found
in the fair one's place,
Bound there upon her bed.

Yet nearer morning | Bray
I went, once more, -
the housefolk slept in the hall,
but soon I found a barking dog
tied fast to that fair maid's couch.

Verse 102 Old Norse

Mörg er góð mær
ef görva kannar
hugbrigð við hali
þá ek þat reynda
er it ráðspaka
teygða ek á flærðir fljóð
háðungar hverrar
leitaði mér it horska man
ok hafða ek þess vættki vífs

Thorpe

Many a fair maiden,
when rightly known,
towards men is fickle:
that I experienced,
when that discreet maiden
I strove to seduce:
contumely of every kind
that wily girl heaped upon me;
nor of that damsel gained I aught.

Bellows Verse 102

"Few are so good
that false they are never
To cheat the mind of a man."
Many fair maids,
if a man but tries them,
False to a lover are found;
That did I learn
when I longed to gain
With wiles the maiden wise;
Foul scorn was my mead
from the crafty maid,
And nought
from the woman I won.

Bray

Many a sweet maid
when one knows her mind
is fickle found towards men:
I proved it well
when that prudent lass
I sought to lead astray:
shrewd maid,
she sought me with every insult
and I won therewith no wife.

Verse 103 Old Norse

Heima glaðr gumi
ok við gesti reifr
sviðr skal um sik vera
minnigr ok málugr
ef hann vill margfróðr vera
opt skal góðs geta
fimbulfambi heitir
sá er fátt kann segja
þat er ósnotrs aðal

Thorpe

At home let a man be cheerful,
and towards a guest liberal;
of wise conduct he should be,
of good memory
and ready speech;
if much knowledge he desires,
he must often talk on good.
Fimbulfambi he is called
who little has to say:
such is the nature of the simple.

Though glad at home, — Bellows Verse 103
and merry with guests,
A man shall be wary and wise;
The sage and shrewd,
wide wisdom seeking,
Must see that his speech be fair;
A fool is he named
who nought can say,
For such is the way of the witless.

In your home be joyous — Bray
and generous to guests
discreet shall you be
in your bearing,
mindful and talkative,
would you gain wisdom,
often making me mention of good.
He is "Simpleton" named
who has nothing to say,
for such is the fashion of fools.

Verse 104 Old Norse

Inn aldna jötum ek sótta
nú em ek aptr um kominn
fátt gat ek þegjandi þar
mörgum orðum
mælta ek í minn frama
í Suttungs sölum

Thorpe

The old Jotun I sought;
now I am come back:
little got I there by silence;
in many words
I spoke to my advantage
in Suttung's halls.

I found the old giant, Bellows Verse
now back have I fared, 104
Small gain from silence I got;
Full many a word,
my will to get,
I spoke in Suttung's hall.

I sought that old Jotun, Bray
now safe am I back,
little served my silence there;
but whispering
many soft speeches
I won my desire
in Suttung's halls.

Verse 105 Old Norse

Gunnlöð mér um gaf
gullnum stóli á
drykk ins dýra mjaðar
ill iðgjöld
lét ek hana eptir hafa
síns ins heila hugar
síns ins svára sefa

Thorpe

Gunnlod gave me,
on her golden seat,
a draught of the precious mead;
a bad recompense
I afterwards made her,
for her whole soul,
her fervent love.

Gunnloth gave on a golden stool Bellows Verse
A drink of the marvellous mead; 105
A harsh reward did I let her have
For her heroic heart,
And her spirit troubled sore.

It was Gunnlod who gave me Bray
on a golden throne
a draught of the glorious mead,
but with poor reward
did I pay her back
for her true and troubled heart.

| Verse 106 | Old Norse | Rata munn<br>létumk rúms um fá<br>ok um grjót gnaga<br>yfir ok undir<br>stóðumk jötna vegir<br>svá hætta ek höfði til |
|---|---|---|
| | Thorpe | Rati's mouth<br>I caused to make a space,<br>and to gnaw the rock;<br>over and under me<br>were the Jotun's ways:<br>thus I my head did peril. |

The mouth of Rati Bellows Verse
made room for my passage, 106
And space in the stone
he gnawed;
Above and below
the giants' paths lay,
So rashly I risked my head.

I bored me a road there Bray
with Rati's tusk
and made room to pass
through the rock;
while the ways of the Jotuns
stretched over and under,
I dared my life for a draught.

Verse 107 — Old Norse

Vel keypts litar
hefi ek vel notit
fás er fróðum vant
því at Óðrerir
er nú upp kominn
á alda vés jarðar

Thorpe

Of a well-assumed form
I made good use:
few things fail the wise;
for Odhrærir
is now come up
to men's earthly dwellings.

Bellows Verse 107

The well-earned beauty
well I enjoyed,
Little the wise man lacks;
So Othrorir now
has up been brought
To the midst of the men of earth.

Bray

In a wily disguise
I worked my will;
little is lacking to the wise,
for the Soul-stirrer now,
sweet Mead of Song,
is brought to men's earthly abode.

Verse 108 Old Norse

Ifi er mér á
at ek væra enn kominn
jötna görðum ór
ef ek Gunnlaðar ne nytak
innar góðu konu
þeirar er lögðumk arm yfir

Thorpe

'Tis to me doubtful
that I could have come
from the Jotun's courts,
had not Gunnlod aided me,
that good damsel,
over whom I laid my arm.

Hardly, methinks, — Bellows Verse 108
would I home have come,
And left the giants' land,
Had not Gunnloth helped me,
the maiden good,
Whose arms about me had been.

I misdoubt me — Bray
if ever again I had come
from the realms of the Jotun race,
had I not served me of Gunnlod,
sweet woman,
her whom I held in mine arms.

Verse 109 | Old Norse

Ins hindra dags
gengu hrímþursar
Háva ráðs at fregna
Háva höllu í
at Bölverki þeir spurðu
ef hann væri með böndum
kominn
eða hefði honum Suttungr of sóit

Thorpe

On the day following
came the Hrimthursar,
to learn something
of the High One,
in the High One's hall:
after Bolverk they inquired,
whether he with the gods
were come,
or Suttung had destroyed him?

The day that followed, Bellows Verse
the frost-giants came, 109
Some word of Hor to win,
(And into the hall of Hor;)
Of Bolverk they asked,
were he back midst the gods,
Or had Suttung slain him there?

Came forth, next day, Bray
the dread Frost Giants,
and entered the High One's Hall:
they asked – was the Baleworker
back mid the Powers,
or had Suttung slain him below?

Verse 110 Old Norse

Baugeið Óðinn
hygg ek at unnit hafi
hvat skal hans tryggðum trúa?
Suttung svikinn
hann lét sumbli frá
ok grœtta Gunnlöðu

Thorpe

Óðinn, I believe, a ring-oath gave.
Who in his faith will trust?
Suttung defrauded,
of his drink bereft,
and Gunnlod made to weep!

On his ring swore Óðinn Bellows Verse
the oath, methinks; 110
Who now his troth shall trust?
Suttung's betrayal
he sought with drink,
And Gunnloth to grief he left.

A ring-oath Óðinn Bray
I trow had taken –
how shall one trust his troth?
It was he who stole
the mead from Suttung,
and Gunnlod caused to weep.

Verse Old Mál er at þylja
111 Norse þular stóli á
Urðar brunni at
sá ek ok þagðak
sá ek ok hugðak
hlýdda ek á manna mál

of rúnar heyrða ek dœma
né um ráðum þögþu
Háva höllu at
Háva höllu í
heyrða ek segja svá

Thorpe Time 'tis to discourse
from the preacher's chair.
By the well of Urd I silent sat,
I saw and meditated,
I listened to men's words.

Of runes I heard discourse,
and of things divine,
nor of graving them
were they silent,
nor of sage counsels,
at the High One's hall.
In the High One's hall.
I thus heard say:

It is time to chant Bellows Verse
from the chanter's stool; 111
By the wells of Urth I was,
I saw and was silent,
I saw and thought,
And heard the speech of Hor.

(Of runes heard I words,
nor were counsels wanting,
At the hall of Hor,
In the hall of Hor;
Such was the speech I heard.)

It is time to speak Bray
from the Sage's Seat;
hard by the Well of Weird
I saw and was silent,
I saw and pondered,
I listened to the speech of men.

Of runes they spoke,
and the reading of runes
was little withheld from their lips:
at the High One's hall,
in the High One's hall,
I thus heard the High One say:

Verse 112 Old Norse

Ráðumk þér Loddfáfnir
en þú ráð nemir
njóta mundu ef þú nemr
þér munu góð ef þú getr
nótt þú rísat
nema á njósn sér
eða þú leitir þér innan út staðar

Thorpe

I counsel thee, Loddfafnir,
to take advice:
thou wilt profit if thou takest it.
Rise not at night,
unless to explore,
or art compelled to go out.

I rede thee, Loddfafnir! Bellows Verse
And hear thou my rede,--- 112
Profit thou hast if thou hearest,
Great thy gain if thou learnest:
Rise not at night,
save if news thou seekest,
Or fain to the outhouse wouldst
fare.

I counsel you, Stray-Singer, Bray
accept my counsels,
they will be your boon
if you obey them,
they will work your weal
if you win them:
rise never at night time,
except you are spying
or seekest a spot without.

Verse 113 Old Norse

Ráðumk þér Loddfáfnir
en þú ráð nemir
njóta mundu ef þú nemr
þér munu góð ef þú getr
fjölkunnigri konu
skalattu í faðmi sofa
svá at hon lyki þik liðum

Thorpe

I counsel thee, Loddfafnir,
to take advice,
thou wilt profit if thou takest it.
In an enchantress's embrace
thou mayest not sleep,
so that in her arms she clasp thee.

I rede thee, Loddfafnir! Bellows Verse
And hear thou my rede,-- 113
Profit thou hast if thou hearest,
Great thy gain if thou learnest:
Beware of sleep
on a witch's bosom,
Nor let her limbs ensnare thee.

I counsel you, Stray-Singer, Bray
accept my counsels,
they will be your boon
if you obey them,
they will work your weal
if you win them:
you shall never sleep
in the arms of a sorceress,
lest she should lock your limbs;

Verse 114 — Old Norse

Hon svá gørir
at þú gáir eigi
þings né þjóðans máls
mat þú villat
né mannskis gaman
ferr þú sorgafullr at sofa

Thorpe

She will be the cause
that thou carest not
For Thyng or prince's words;
food thou wilt shun
and human joys;
sorrowful wilt thou go to sleep.

Such is her might
that thou hast no mind
For the council
or meeting of men;
Meat thou hatest,
joy thou hast not,
And sadly to slumber thou farest.

Bellows Verse 114

So shall she charm
that you shall not heed
the council, or words of the king,
nor care for your food,
or the joys of mankind,
but fall into sorrowful sleep.

Bray

Verse 115

Old Norse

Ráðumk þér Loddfáfnir
en þú ráð nemir
njóta mundu ef þú nemr
þér munu góð ef þú getr
annars konu
teygðu þér aldregi
eyrarúnu at

Thorpe

I counsel thee, Loddfafnir,
to take advice
Another's wife
entice thou never
to secret converse.

I rede thee, Loddfafnir! Bellows Verse
And hear thou my rede,-- 115
Profit thou hast if thou hearest,
Great thy gain if thou learnest:
Seek never to win
the wife of another,
Or long for her secret love.

I counsel you, Stray-Singer, Bray
accept my counsels,
they will be your boon
if you obey them,
they will work your weal
if you win them:
seek not ever to draw to yourself
in love-whispering
another's wife.

Verse 116 Old Norse

Ráðumk þér Loddfáfnir
en þú ráð nemir
njóta mundu ef þú nemr
þér munu góð ef þú getr
á fjalli eða firði
ef þik fara tíðir
fásktu at virði vel

Thorpe

I counsel thee, Loddfafnir,
to take advice
By fell or firth
if thou have to travel,
provide thee well with food.

I rede thee, Loddfafnir! Bellows Verse
And hear thou my rede,-- 116
Profit thou hast if thou hearest,
Great thy gain if thou learnest:
If o'er mountains or gulfs
thou fain wouldst go,
Look well to thy food
for the way.

I counsel you, Stray-Singer, Bray
accept my counsels,
they will be your boon
if you obey them,
they will work your weal
if you win them:
should you long to fare
over fell and firth
provide you well with food.

Verse 117 Old Norse

Ráðumk þér Loddfáfnir
en þú ráð nemir
njóta mundu ef þú nemr
þér munu góð ef þú getr
illan mann
láttu aldregi
óhöpp at þér vita
því at af illum manni
fær þú aldregi
gjöld ins góða hugar

Thorpe

I counsel thee, Loddfafnir,
to take advice
A bad man let thou never know
thy misfortunes;
for from a bad man
thou never wilt obtain a return
for thy good will.

Bellows Verse 117

I rede thee, Loddfafnir!
And hear thou my rede,--
Profit thou hast if thou hearest,
Great thy gain if thou learnest:
An evil man thou must not let
Bring aught of ill to thee;
For an evil man will never make
Reward for a worthy thought.

Bray

I counsel you, Stray-Singer,
accept my counsels,
they will be your boon
if you obey them,
they will work your weal
if you win them:
tell not ever an evil man
if misfortunes you befall,
from such ill friend
you need never seek
return for your trustful mind.

Verse 118 | Old Norse

Ofarla bíta
ek sá einum hal
orð illrar konu;
fláráð tunga
varð honum at fjörlagi
ok þeygi um sanna sök

Thorpe

I saw mortally wound a man
a wicked woman's words;
a false tongue caused his death,
and most unrighteously.

I saw a man — Bellows Verse 118
who was wounded sore
By an evil woman's word;
A lying tongue
his death-blow launched,
And no word of truth there was.

Wounded to death, — Bray
have I seen a man
by the words of an evil woman;
a lying tongue
had bereft him of life,
and all without reason of right.

Verse 119 — Old Norse

Ráðumk þér Loddfáfnir
en þú ráð nemir
njóta mundu ef þú nemr
þér munu góð ef þú getr
veiztu ef þú vin átt
þanns þú vel trúir
farðu at finna opt
því at hrísi vex
ok hávu grasi
vegr er vættki trøðr

Thorpe

I counsel thee, Loddfafnir,
to take advice
If thou knowest thou hast a friend,
whom thou well canst trust,
go oft to visit him;
for with brushwood over-grown,
and with high grass,
is the way that no one treads.

I rede thee, Loddfafnir! Bellows Verse
And hear thou my rede,-- 119
Profit thou hast if thou hearest,
Great thy gain if thou learnest:
If a friend thou hast
whom thou fully wilt trust,
Then fare to find him oft;
For brambles grow
and waving grass
On the rarely trodden road.

I counsel you, Stray-Singer, Bray
accept my counsels,
they will be your boon
if you obey them,
they will work your weal
if you win them:
have you a friend
whom you trustest well,
fare you to find him often;
for with brushwood grows
and with grasses high
the path where no foot passes.

Verse 120

Old Norse

Ráðumk þér Loddfáfnir
en þú ráð nemir
njóta mundu ef þú nemr
þér munu góð ef þú getr
góðan mann
teygðu þér at gamanrúnum
ok nem líknargaldr meðan þú lifir

Thorpe

I counsel thee, Loddfafnir,
to take advice
A good man attract to thee
in pleasant converse;
and salutary speech
learn while thou livest.

I rede thee, Loddfafnir! Bellows Verse
And hear thou my rede,-- 120
Profit thou hast if thou hearest,
Great thy gain if thou learnest:
A good man find
to hold in friendship,
And give heed
to his healing charms.

I counsel you, Stray-Singer, Bray
accept my counsels,
they will be your boon
if you obey them,
they will work your weal
if you win them:
in sweet converse
call the righteous
to your side,
learn a healing song
while you live.

Verse Old Ráðumk þér Loddfáfnir
121 Norse en þú ráð nemir
njóta mundu ef þú nemr
þér munu góð ef þú getr
vin þínum
ver þú aldregi
fyrri at flaumslitum
sorg etr hjarta
ef þú segja ne náir
einhverjum allan hug

Thorpe I counsel thee, Loddfafnir,
to take advice
With thy friend
be thou never first to quarrel.
Care gnaws the heart,
if thou to no one
canst thy whole mind disclose.

I rede thee, Loddfafnir! Bellows Verse
And hear thou my rede,- 121
Profit thou hast if thou hearest,
Great thy gain if thou learnest:
Be never the first
to break with thy friend
The bond that holds you both;
Care eats the heart
if thou canst not speak
To another all thy thought.

I counsel you, Stray-Singer, Bray
accept my counsels,
they will be your boon
if you obey them,
they will work your weal
if you win them:
be never the first
with friend of thine
to break the bond of fellowship;
care shall gnaw your heart
if you cannot tell
all your mind to another.

Verse 122 — Old Norse

Ráðumk þér Loddfáfnir
en þú ráð nemir
njóta mundu ef þú nemr
þér munu góð ef þú getr
orðum skipta
þú skalt aldregi
við ósvinna apa

Thorpe

I counsel thee, Loddfafnir,
to take advice
Words thou never
shouldst exchange
with a witless fool;

I rede thee, Loddfafnir! Bellows Verse
And hear thou my rede,-- 122
Profit thou hast if thou hearest,
Great thy gain if thou learnest:
Exchange of words
with a witless ape
Thou must not ever make.

I counsel you, Stray-Singer, Bray
accept my counsels,
they will be your boon
if you obey them,
they will work your weal
if you win them:
never in speech
with a foolish knave
should you waste a single word.

Verse 123 Old Norse

því at af illum manni
mundu aldregi
góðs laun um geta
en góðr maðr
mun þik gørva mega
líknfastan at lofi

Thorpe

For from an ill-conditioned man
thou wilt never
get a return for good;
but a good man
will bring thee favour
by his praise.

Bellows Verse 123

For never thou mayst
from an evil man
A good requital get;
But a good man
oft the greatest love
Through words of praise
will win thee.

Bray

From the lips of such
you need not look
for reward of thine
own good will;
but a righteous man by praise
will render you firm
in favour and love.

Verse 124 Old Norse

Sifjum er þá blandat
hverr er segja ræðr
einum allan hug
alt er betra
en sé brigðum at vera
era sá vinr öðrum
er vilt eitt segir

Thorpe

There is a mingling of affection,
where one can tell
another all his mind.
Everything is better
than being with the deceitful.
He is not another's friend
who ever says as he says.

Bellows Verse 124

Mingled is love
when a man can speak
To another all his thought;
Nought is so bad as false to be,
No friend speaks only fair.

Bray

There is mingling in friendship
when man can utter
all his whole mind to another;
there is nothing so vile
as a fickle tongue;
no friend is he who but flatters.

Verse 125 Old Norse

Ráðumk þér Loddfáfnir
en þú ráð nemir
njóta mundu ef þú nemr
þér munu góð ef þú getr
þrimr orðum senna
skalattu þér við verra mann
opt inn betri bilar
þá er inn verri vegr

Thorpe

I counsel thee, Loddfafnir,
to take advice
Even in three words
quarrel not with a worse man:
often the better yields,
when the worse strikes.

I rede thee, Loddfafnir! Bellows Verse
And hear thou my rede,-- 125
Profit thou hast if thou hearest,
Great thy gain if thou learnest:
With a worse man
speak not three words in dispute,
Ill fares the better oft
When the worse man
wields a sword.

I counsel you, Stray-Singer, Bray
accept my counsels,
they will be your boon
if you obey them,
they will work your weal
if you win them:
often the worst
lays the best one low.

Verse 126 Old Norse

Ráðumk þér Loddfáfnir
en þú ráð nemir
njóta mundu ef þú nemr
þér munu góð ef þú getr
skósmiðr þú verir
né skeptismiðr
nema þú sjálfum þér sér
skór er skapaðr illa
eða skapt sé rangt
þá er þér böls beðit

Thorpe

I counsel thee, Loddfafnir,
to take advice
Be not a shoemaker,
nor a shaftmaker,
unless for thyself it be;
for a shoe if ill made,
or a shaft if crooked,
will call down evil on thee.

I rede thee, Loddfafnir! Bellows Verse 126
And hear thou my rede,-
Profit thou hast if thou hearest,
Great thy gain if thou learnest:
A shoemaker be,
or a maker of shafts,
For only thy single self;
If the shoe is ill made,
or the shaft prove false,
Then evil of thee men think.

I counsel you, Stray-Singer, Bray
accept my counsels,
they will be your boon
if you obey them,
they will work your weal
if you win them:
be not a shoemaker
nor yet a shaft maker
save for yourself alone:
let the shoe be misshapen,
or crooked the shaft,
and a curse on your head
will be called.

Verse Old Ráðumk þér Loddfáfnir
127 Norse en þú ráð nemir
njóta mundu ef þú nemr
þér munu góð ef þú getr
hvars þú böl kannt
kveðu þat bölvi at
ok gefat þínum fjándum frið

Thorpe I counsel thee, Loddfafnir,
to take advice
Wherever of injury
thou knowest,
regard that injury as thy own;
and give to thy foes no peace.

I rede thee, Loddfafnir! Bellows Verse
And hear thou my rede,-- 127
Profit thou hast if thou hearest,
Great thy gain if thou learnest:
If evil thou knowest,
as evil proclaim it,
And make no friendship
with foes.

I counsel you, Stray-Singer, Bray
accept my counsels,
they will be your boon
if you obey them,
they will work your weal
if you win them:
when in peril you see you,
confess you in peril,
nor ever give peace to your foes.

Verse 128 Old Norse

Ráðumk þér Loddfáfnir
en þú ráð nemir
njóta mundu ef þú nemr
þér munu góð ef þú getr
illu feginn
verðu aldregi
en lát þér at góðu getit

Thorpe

I counsel thee, Loddfafnir,
to take advice
Rejoiced at evil be thou never;
but let good give thee pleasure.

I rede thee, Loddfafnir! Bellows Verse
And hear thou my rede,-- 128
Profit thou hast if thou hearest,
Great thy gain if thou learnest:
In evil never joy shalt thou know,
But glad the good shall make thee.

I counsel you, Stray-Singer, Bray
accept my counsels,
they will be your boon
if you obey them,
they will work your
weal if you win them:
rejoice not ever at tidings of ill,
but glad let your soul be in good.

Verse 129 Old Norse

Ráðumk þér Loddfáfnir
en þú ráð nemir
njóta mundu ef þú nemr
þér munu góð ef þú getr
upp líta
skalattu í orrostu
gjalti glíkir
verða gumna synir
síðr þitt um heilli halir

Thorpe

I counsel thee, Loddfafnir,
to take advice
In a battle look not up,
(like swine
the sons of men then become)
that men may not fascinate thee.

I rede thee, Loddfafnir! Bellows Verse
And hear thou my rede,-- 129
Profit thou hast if thou hearest,
Great thy gain if thou learnest:
Look not up
when the battle is on,--
(Like madmen
the sons of men become,--)
Lest men bewitch thy wits.

I counsel you, Stray-Singer, Bray
accept my counsels,
they will be your boon
if you obey them,
they will work your weal
if you win them:
look not up in battle,
when men are as beasts,
lest the wights
bewitch you with spells.

Verse 130 Old Norse

Ráðumk þér Loddfáfnir
en þú ráð nemir
njóta mundu ef þú nemr
þér munu góð ef þú getr
ef þú vilt þér góða konu
kveðja at gamanrúnum
ok fá fögnuð af
fögru skaltu heita
ok láta fast vera
leiðisk manngi gott, ef getr

Thorpe

I counsel thee, Loddfafnir,
to take advice
If thou wilt induce a good woman
to pleasant converse,
thou must promise fair,
and hold to it:
no one turns from good
if it can be got.

I rede thee, Loddfafnir! Bellows Verse
And hear thou my rede,- 130
Profit thou hast if thou hearest,
Great thy gain if thou learnest:
If thou fain wouldst win
a woman's love,
And gladness get from her,
Fair be thy promise
and well fulfilled;
None loathes what good he gets.

I counsel you, Stray-Singer, Bray
accept my counsels,
they will be your boon
if you obey them,
they will work your weal
if you win them:
would you win joy
of a gentle maiden,
and lure to whispering of love,
make fair promise,
and let it be fast, -
none will scorn their weal
who can win it.

Verse 131 Old Norse

Ráðumk þér Loddfáfnir
en þú ráð nemir
njóta mundu ef þú nemr
þér munu góð ef þú getr
varan bið ek þik vera
en eigi ofvaran
ver þú við öl varastr
ok við annars konu
ok við þat it þriðja
at þjófar ne leiki

Thorpe

I counsel thee, Loddfafnir,
to take advice
I enjoin thee to be wary,
but not over wary;
at drinking be thou most wary,
and with another's wife;
and thirdly,
that thieves delude thee not.

I rede thee, Loddfafnir! Bellows Verse
And hear thou my rede,- 131
Profit thou hast if thou hearest,
Great thy gain if thou learnest:
I bid thee be wary,
but be not fearful;
(Beware most with ale
or another's wife,
And third beware
lest a thief outwit thee.)

I counsel you, Stray-Singer, Bray
accept my counsels,
they will be your boon
if you obey them,
they will work your weal
if you win them:
I pray you be wary,
yet not too wary,
be wariest of all with ale,
with another's wife,
and a third thing eke,
that knaves outwit you never.

Verse 132 Old Norse

Ráðumk þér Loddfáfnir
en þú ráð nemir
njóta mundu ef þú nemr
þér munu góð ef þú getr
at háði né hlátri
hafðu aldregi
gest né ganganda

Thorpe

I counsel thee, Loddfafnir,
to take advice
With insult or derision
treat thou never
a guest or wayfarer.
They often little know,
who sit within,
of what race they are who come.

I rede thee, Loddfafnir! Bellows Verse
And hear thou my rede,- 132
Profit thou hast if thou hearest,
Great thy gain if thou learnest:
Scorn or mocking
ne'er shalt thou make
Of a guest or a journey-goer.

I counsel you, Stray-Singer, Bray
accept my counsels,
they will be your boon
if you obey them,
they will work your weal
if you win them:
hold not in scorn,
nor mock in your halls
a guest or wandering wight.

| | | |
|---|---|---|
| Verse 133 | Old Norse | Opt vitu ógörla<br>þeir er sitja inni fyrir<br>hvers þeir ro kyns er koma<br>erat maðr svá góðr<br>at galli ne fylgi<br>né svá illr at einugi dugi |
| | Thorpe | Vices and virtues<br>the sons of mortals bear<br>in their breasts mingled;<br>no one is so good<br>that no failing attends him,<br>nor so bad<br>as to be good for nothing. |

Oft scarcely he knows Bellows Verse
who sits in the house 133
What kind is the man who comes;
None so good is found
that faults he has not,
Nor so wicked
that nought he is worth.

They know but unsurely Bray
who sit within
what kind of man is come:
none is found so good,
but some fault attends him,
or so ill
but he serves for somewhat.

Verse 134 Old Norse

Ráðumk þér Loddfáfnir
en þú ráð nemir
njóta mundu ef þú nemr
þér munu góð ef þú getr
at hárum þul
hlæðu aldregi
opt er gott þat er gamlir kveða
opt ór skörpum belg
skilin orð koma
þeim er hangir með hám
ok skollir með skrám
ok váfir með vílmögum

Thorpe

I counsel thee, Loddfafnir,
to take advice
At a hoary speaker
laugh thou never;
often is good
that which the aged utter,
oft from a shriveled hide
discreet words issue;
from those whose skin is pendent
and decked with scars,
and who go tottering
among the vile.

I rede thee, Loddfafnir! Bellows Verse
And hear thou my rede,-- 134
Profit thou hast if thou hearest,
Great thy gain if thou learnest:
Scorn not ever
the gray-haired singer,
Oft do the old speak good;
(Oft from shrivelled skin
come skillful counsels,
Though it hang with the hides,
And flap with the pelts,
And is blown with the bellies.)

I counsel you, Stray-Singer, Bray
accept my counsels,
they will be your boon
if you obey them,
they will work your weal
if you win them:
hold never in scorn
the hoary singer;
often the counsel
of the old is good;
come words of wisdom
from the withered lips
of him left to hang among hides,
to rock with the rennets
and swing with the skins.

Verse 135 Old Norse

Ráðumk þér Loddfáfnir
en þú ráð nemir
njóta mundu ef þú nemr
þér munu góð ef þú getr
gest þú ne geyja
né á grind hrekir
get þú váluðum vel

Thorpe

I counsel thee, Loddfafnir,
to take advice
Rail not at a guest,
nor from thy gate thrust him;
treat well the indigent;
they will speak well of thee.

I rede thee, Loddfafnir! Bellows Verse 135
And hear thou my rede,--
Profit thou hast if thou hearest,
Great thy gain if thou learnest:
Curse not thy guest,
nor show him thy gate,
Deal well with a man in want.

I counsel you, Stray-Singer, Bray
accept my counsels,
they will be your boon
if you obey them,
they will work your weal
if you win them:
growl not at guests,
nor drive them from the gate
but show yourself
gentle to the poor.

| | | |
|---|---|---|
| Verse 136 | Old Norse | Rammt er þat tré<br>er ríða skal<br>öllum at upploki<br>baug þú gef<br>eða þat biðja mun<br>þér læs hvers á liðu |
| | Thorpe | Strong is the bar<br>that must be raised to admit all.<br>Do thou give a penny,<br>or they will call down on thee<br>every ill in thy limbs. |

Strong is the beam
that raised must be
To give an entrance to all;
Give it a ring, or grim will be
The wish it would work on thee.

Bellows Verse
136

Mighty is the bar
to be moved away
for the entering in of all.
Shower your wealth,
or men shall wish you
every ill in your limbs.

Bray

Verse 137 Old Norse

Ráðumk þér Loddfáfnir
en þú ráð nemir
njóta mundu ef þú nemr
þér munu góð ef þú getr
hvars þú öl drekkr
kjós þú þér jarðar megin
því at jörð tekr við ölðri
en eldr við sóttum.
eik við abbindi,
ax við fjölkynngi
höll við hýrógi
– heiptum skal mana kveðja –
beiti við bitsóttum,
en við bölvi runar;
fold skal við flóði taka.

Thorpe

I counsel thee, Loddfafnir,
to take advice:-
Wherever thou beer drinkest,
invoke to thee the power of earth;
for earth is good against drink,
fire for distempers,
the oak for constipation,
a corn-ear for sorcery,
a hall for domestic strife.
In bitter hates invoke the moon;
the biter for bite-injuries is good;
but runes against calamity;
fluid let earth absorb.

I rede thee, Loddfafnir! Bellows Verse 137
And hear thou my rede,--
Profit thou hast if thou hearest,
Great thy gain if thou learnest:
When ale thou drunkest
seek might of earth,
(For earth cures drink,
and fire cures ills,
The oak cures tightness,
the ear cures magic,
Rye cures rupture,
the moon cures rage,
Grass cures the scab,
and runes the sword-cut;)
The field absorbs the flood.

I counsel you, Stray-Singer, Bray
accept my counsels,
they will be your boon
if you obey them,
they will work your weal
if you win them:
when ale you quaffest,
call upon earth's might –
it is earth drinks in the floods.
Earth prevails over drink,
but fire over sickness, the oak
over binding, the earcorn over
witchcraft, the rye spur over
rupture, the moon over rages,
herb over cattle plagues,
runes over harm.

Verse 138 — Old Norse

Veit ek at ek hekk
vindga meiði á
nætr allar níu
geiri undaðr
ok gefinn Óðni
sjálfr sjálfum mér
á þeim meiði
er manngi veit
hvers hann af rótum renn

Thorpe

I know that I hung,
on a wind-rocked tree,
nine whole nights,
with a spear wounded,
and to Óðinn offered,
myself to myself;
on that tree,
of which no one knows
from what root it springs.

I ween that I hung — Bellows Verse 138
on the windy tree,
Hung there for nights full nine;
With the spear I was wounded,
and offered I was
To Óðinn, myself to myself,
On the tree
that none may ever know
What root beneath it runs.

I trow I hung on that windy Tree — Bray
nine whole days and nights,
stabbed with a spear,
offered to Óðinn,
myself to mine own self given,
high on that Tree
of which none has heard
from what roots it rises to heaven.

Verse 139 Old Norse

Við hleifi mik sældu
né við hornigi
nýsta ek niðr
nam ek upp rúnar
œpandi nam
fell ek aptr þaðan

Thorpe

Bread no one gave me,
nor a horn of drink,
downward I peered,
to runes applied myself,
wailing learnt them,
then fell down thence.

Bellows Verse 139

None made me happy
with loaf or horn,
And there below I looked;
I took up the runes,
shrieking I took them,
And forthwith back I fell.

Bray

None refreshed me ever
with food or drink,
I peered right down in the deep;
crying aloud I lifted the Runes
then back I fell from thence.

Verse 140

Old Norse

Fimbulljóð níu
nam ek af inum frægja syni
Bölþórs Bestlu föður
ok ek drykk of gat
ins dýra mjaðar
ausinn Óðreri

Thorpe

Potent songs nine
from the famed son
I learned of Bolthorn,
Bestla's sire,
and a draught obtained
of the precious mead,
drawn from Odhrærir.

Nine mighty songs Bellows Verse
I got from the son 140
Of Bolthorn, Bestla's father;
And a drink I got
of the goodly mead
Poured out from Othrorir.

Nine mighty songs Bray
I learned from the great son
of Bale-thorn, Bestla's sire;
I drank a measure
of the wondrous Mead,
with the Soulstirrer's drops
I was showered.

Verse 141 Old Norse

Þá nam ek frævask
ok fróðr vera
ok vaxa ok vel hafask
orð mér af orði
orðs leitaði
verk mér af verki
verks leitaði

Thorpe

Then I began to bear fruit,
and to know many things,
to grow and well thrive:
word by word
I sought out words,
fact by fact
I sought out facts.

Then began I to thrive, Bellows Verse
and wisdom to get, 141
I grew and well I was;
Each word led me on
to another word,
Each deed to another deed.

Before long I bare fruit, Bray
and throve full well,
I grew and waxed in wisdom;
word following word,
I found me words,
deed following deed,
I wrought deeds.

Verse 142 | Old Norse

Rúnar munt þú finna
ok ráðna stafi
mjök stóra stafi
mjök stinna stafi
er fáði fimbulþulr
ok gørðu ginnregin
ok reist Hroptr rögna

Thorpe

Runes thou wilt find,
and explained characters,
very large characters,
very potent characters,
which the great speaker depicted,
and the high powers formed,
and the powers' prince graved:

Runes shalt thou find, Bellows Verse 142
and fateful signs,
That the king of singers coloured,
And the mighty gods have made;
Full strong the signs,
full mighty the signs
That the ruler of gods doth write.

Hidden Runes shall you seek Bray
and interpreted signs,
many symbols
of might and power,
by the great Singer painted,
by the high Powers fashioned,
graved by the Utterer of gods.

Verse 143

Old Norse

Óðinn með ásum
en fyr álfum Dáinn
ok Dvalinn dvergum fyrir
Ásviðr jötnum fyrir
ek reist sjálfr sumar

Thorpe

Óðinn among the Æsir,
but among the Alfar, Dain,
and Dvalin for the dwarfs,
Asvid for the Jotuns:
some I myself graved.

Óðinn for the gods, Bellows Verse 143
Dain for the elves,
And Dvalin for the dwarfs,
Alsvith for giants
and all mankind,
And some myself I wrote.

For gods graved Óðinn, Bray
for elves graved Dan,
Dvalin the Dallier for dwarfs,
All-wise for Jotuns,
and I, of myself,
graved some for the sons of men.

Verse 144 Old Norse

Veiztu hvé rísta skal?
Veiztu hvé ráða skal?
Veiztu hvé fá skal?
Veiztu hvé freista skal?
Veiztu hvé biðja skal?
Veiztu hvé blóta skal?
Veiztu hvé senda skal?
Veiztu hvé sóa skal?

Thorpe

Knowest thou
how to grave them?
Knowest thou
how to expound them?
Knowest thou
how to depict them?
Knowest thou
how to prove them?
Knowest thou
how to pray?
Knowest thou
how to offer?
Knowest thou
how to send?
Knowest thou
how to consume?

Bellows Verse 144

Knowest how one shall write,
knowest how one shall rede?
Knowest how one shall tint,
knowest how one makes trial?
Knowest how one shall ask,
knowest how one shall offer?
Knowest how one shall send,
knowest how one shall sacrifice?

Bray

Do you now how to write,
know how to read,
know how to paint,
know how to prove,
know how to ask,
know how to offer,
know how to send,
know how to spend?

Verse 145 Old Norse

Betra er óbeðit
en sé ofblótit
ey sér til gildis gjöf
betra er ósent
en sé ofsóit
svá Þundr um reist
fyr þjóða rök
þar hann upp um reis
er hann aptr of kom

Thorpe

'Tis better not to pray
than too much offer;
a gift ever looks to a return.
'Tis better not to send
than too much consume.
So Thund graved
before the origin of men,
where he ascended,
to whence he afterwards came.

Better no prayer | Bellows Verse
than too big an offering, | 145
By thy getting measure thy gift;
Better is none
than too big a sacrifice,
So Thund of old wrote
ere man's race began,
Where he rose on high
when home he came.

Better ask for too little | Bray
than offer too much,
like the gift should be the boon;
better not to spend
than to overspend.
Thus Óðinn graved
before the world began;
Then he rose from the deep,
and came again.

Verse 146 Old Norse

Ljóð ek þau kann
er kannat þjóðans kona
ok mannskis mögr
hjálp heitir eitt
en þat þér hjálpa mun
við sökum ok sorgum
ok sútum görvöllum

Thorpe

Those songs I know
which the king's wife knows not
nor son of man.
Help the first is called,
for that will help thee
against strifes and cares.

The songs I know Bellows Verse 146
that king's wives know not,
Nor men that are sons of men;
The first is called help,
and help it can bring thee
In sorrow and pain and sickness.

Those songs I know, Bray
which nor sons of men nor queen
in a king's court knows;
the first is Help
which will bring you help
in all woes and in sorrow and
strife.

| | | |
|---|---|---|
| Verse 147 | Old Norse | Þat kann ek annat<br>er þurfu ýta synir<br>þeir er vilja læknar lifa |

| | |
|---|---|
| Thorpe | For the second I know,<br>what the sons of men require,<br>who will as leeches live. |

A second I know, Bellows Verse 147
that men shall need
Who leechcraft long to use;

A second I know, Bray
which the son of men must sing,
who would heal the sick.

Verse 148 Old Norse

Þat kann ek it þriðja
ef mér verðr þörf mikil
hapts við mína heiptmögu
eggjar ek deyfi
minna andskota
bítat þeim vápn né velir

Thorpe

For the third I know,
if I have great need
to restrain my foes,
the weapons' edge I deaden:
of my adversaries
nor arms nor wiles harm aught.

A third I know, Bellows Verse 148
if great is my need
Of fetters to hold my foe;
Blunt do I make
mine enemy's blade,
Nor bites his sword or staff.

A third I know: Bray
if sore need should come
of a spell to stay my foes;
when I sing that song,
which shall blunt their swords,
nor their weapons
nor staves can wound.

Verse 149

Old Norse

Þat kann ek it fjórða
ef mér fyrðar bera
bönd at bóglimum
svá ek gel
at ek ganga má
sprettr mér af fótum fjöturr
en af höndum hapt

Thorpe

For the fourth I know,
if men place bonds on my limbs,
I so sing that I can walk;
the fetter starts from my feet,
and the manacle from my hands.

A fourth I know, Bellows Verse
if men shall fasten 149
Bonds on my bended legs;
So great is the charm
that forth I may go,
The fetters spring from my feet,
Broken the bonds from my hands.

A fourth I know: Bray
if men make fast
in chains the joints of my limbs,
when I sing that song
which shall set me free,
spring the fetters
from hands and feet.

Verse 150

Old Norse

Þat kann ek it fimmta
ef ek sé af fári skotinn
flein í fólki vaða
flýgra hann svá stinnt
at ek stöðvigak
ef ek hann sjónum of sék

Thorpe

For the fifth I know,
if I see a shot from a hostile hand,
a shaft flying amid the host,
so swift it cannot fly
that I cannot arrest it,
if only I get sight of it.

A fifth I know, Bellows Verse
if I see from afar 150
An arrow fly 'gainst the folk;
It flies not so swift
that I stop it not,
If ever my eyes behold it.

A fifth I know: Bray
when I see, by foes shot,
speeding a shaft through the host,
flies it never so strongly
I still can stay it,
if I get but a glimpse of its flight.

Verse 151 Old Norse

Þat kann ek it sétta
ef mik særir þegn
á rótum rams viðar
ok þann hal
er mik heipta kveðr
þann eta mein heldr en mik

Thorpe

For the sixth I know,
if one wounds me
with a green tree's roots;
also if a man declares hatred to me,
harm shall consume them
sooner than me.

Bellows Verse 151

A sixth I know,
if harm one seeks
With a sapling's roots to send me;
The hero himself
who wreaks his hate
Shall taste the ill ere I.

Bray

A sixth I know:
when some thane
would harm me
in runes on a moist tree's root,
on his head alone
shall light the ills
of the curse
that he called upon mine.

Verse 152 Old Norse

Þat kann ek it sjaunda
ef ek sé hávan loga
sal um sessmögum
brennrat svá breitt
at ek honum bjargigak
þann kann ek galdr at gala

Thorpe

For the seventh I know,
if a lofty house I see
blaze o'er its inmates,
so furiously it shall not burn
that I cannot save it.
That song I can sing.

A seventh I know, Bellows Verse
if I see in flames 152
The hall o'er my comrades' heads;
It burns not so wide
that I will not quench it,
I know that song to sing.

A seventh I know: Bray
if I see a hall high over
the bench-mates blazing,
flame it never so fiercely
I still can save it, -
I know how to sing that song.

Verse 153 Old Norse

Þat kann ek it átta
er öllum er
nytsamligt at nema
hvars hatr vex
með hildings sonum
þat má ek bœta brátt

Thorpe

For the eighth I know,
what to all is useful to learn:
where hatred grows
among the sons of men
--that I can quickly assuage.

An eighth I know, Bellows Verse
that is to all 153
Of greatest good to learn;
When hatred grows
among heroes' sons,
I soon can set it right.

An eighth I know: Bray
which all can sing
for their weal
if they learn it well;
where hate shall wax
'mid the warrior sons,
I can calm it soon with that song.

Verse 154

Old Norse

Þat kann ek it níunda
ef mik nauðr um stendr
at bjarga fari mínu á floti
vind ek kyrri
vági á
ok svæfik allan sæ

Thorpe

For the ninth I know,
if I stand in need
my bark on the water to save,
I can the wind
on the waves allay,
and the sea lull.

A ninth I know, Bellows Verse
if need there comes 154
To shelter my ship on the flood;
The wind I calm upon the waves,
And the sea I put to sleep.

A ninth I know: Bray
when need befalls me
to save my vessel afloat,
I hush the wind
on the stormy wave,
and soothe all the sea to rest.

Verse 155 Old Norse

Þat kann ek it tíunda
ef ek sé túnriðir
leika lopti á
ek svá vinnk
at þeir villir fara
sinna heimhama
sinna heimhuga

Thorpe

For the tenth I know,
if I see troll-wives sporting in air,
I can so operate
that they will forsake
their own forms,
and their own minds.

A tenth I know, Bellows Verse
what time I see 155
House-riders flying on high;
So can I work that wildly they go,
Showing their true shapes,
Hence to their own homes.

A tenth I know: Bray
when at night the witches
ride and sport in the air,
such spells I weave
that they wander home
out of skins and wits bewildered.

Verse 156 Old Norse

Þat kann ek it ellipta
ef ek skal til orrostu
leiða langvini
undir randir ek gel
en þeir með ríki fara
heilir hildar til
heilir hildi frá
koma þeir heilir hvaðan

Thorpe

For the eleventh I know,
if I have to lead
my ancient friends to battle,
under their shields I sing,
and with power
they go safe to the fight,
safe from the fight;
safe on every side they go.

An eleventh I know, Bellows Verse
if needs I must lead to the fight 156
my long-loved friends;
I sing in the shields,
and in strength they go
Whole to the field of fight,
Whole from the field of fight,
And whole they come
thence home.

An eleventh I know: Bray
if haply I lead
my old comrades out to war,
I sing 'neath the shields,
and they fare forth mightily
safe into battle,
safe out of battle,
and safe return from the strife.

Verse 157 Old Norse

Þat kann ek it tólpta
ef ek sé á tré uppi
váfa virgilná
svá ek ríst
ok í rúnum fák
at sá gengr gumi
ok mælir við mik

Thorpe

For the twelfth I know,
if on a tree I see a corpse
swinging from a halter,
I can so grave and in runes depict,
that the man shall walk,
and with me converse.

A twelfth I know, Bellows Verse
if high on a tree 157
I see a hanged man swing;
So do I write and colour the runes
That forth he fares,
And to me talks.

A twelfth I know: Bray
if I see in a tree
a corpse from a halter hanging,
such spells I write,
and paint in runes,
that the being descends
and speaks.

Verse 158 Old Norse

Þat kann ek it þrettánda
ef ek skal þegn ungan
verpa vatni á
munat hann falla
þótt hann í fólk komi
hnígra sá halr fyr hjörum

Thorpe

For the thirteenth I know,
if on a young man
I sprinkle water,
he shall not fall,
though he into battle come
that man shall not sink
before swords.

A thirteenth I know, Bellows Verse 158
if a thane full young
With water I sprinkle well;
He shall not fall,
though he fares mid the host,
Nor sink beneath the swords.

A thirteenth I know: Bray
if the new-born son of a warrior
I sprinkle with water,
that youth will not fail
when he fares to war,
never slain
shall he bow before sword.

Verse 159 Old Norse

Þat kann ek it fjórtánda
ef ek skal fyrða liði
telja tíva fyrir
ása ok álfa
ek kann allra skil
fár kann ósnotr svá

Thorpe

For the fourteenth I know,
if in the society of men
I have to enumerate the gods,
Æsir and Alfar,
I know the distinctions of all.
This few unskilled can do.

A fourteenth I know, Bellows Verse
if fain I would name 159
To men the mighty gods;
All know I well
of the gods and elves,
Few be the fools know this.

A fourteenth I know: Bray
if I needs must number
the Powers to the people of men,
I know all the nature
of gods and of elves
which none can know untaught.

Verse 160 Old Norse

Þat kann ek it fimmtánda
er gól Þjóðreyrir
dvergr fyr Dellings durum
afl gól hann ásum
en álfum frama
hyggju Hroptatý

Thorpe

For the fifteenth I know
what the dwarf Thiodreyrir sang
before Delling's doors.
Strength he sang to the Æsir,
and to the Alfar prosperity,
wisdom to Hroptatyr.

A fifteenth I know, Bellows Verse
that before the doors 160
Of Delling sang
Thjothrorir the dwarf;
Might he sang for the gods,
and glory for elves,
And wisdom for Hroptatyr wise.

A fifteenth I know, Bray
which Folk-stirrer sang,
the dwarf, at the gates of Dawn;
he sang strength to the gods,
and skill to the elves,
and wisdom to Óðinn who utters.

Verse 161 — Old Norse

Þat kann ek it sextánda
ef ek vil ins svinna mans
hafa geð alt ok gaman
hugi ek hverfi
hvítarmri konu
ok snÿ ek hennar öllum sefa

Thorpe

For the sixteenth I know,
if a modest maiden's favour
and affection
I desire to possess,
the soul I change
of the white-armed damsel,
and wholly turn her mind.

A sixteenth I know, Bellows Verse
if I seek delight 161
To win from a maiden wise;
The mind I turn
of the white-armed maid,
And thus change all her thoughts.

A sixteenth I know: Bray
when all sweetness and love
I would win
from some artful wench,
her heart I turn,
and the whole mind change
of that fair-armed lady I love.

Verse 162 Old Norse

Þat kann ek it sjautjánda
at mik mun seint firrask
it manunga man
ljóða þessa
mun þú Loddfáfnir
lengi vanr vera
þó sé þér góð ef þú getr
nýt ef þú nemr
þörf ef þú þiggr

Thorpe

For the seventeenth I know,
that that young maiden
will reluctantly avoid me.

These songs,
Loddfafnir!
Thou wilt long have lacked;
yet it may be good
if thou understandest them,
profitable if thou learnest them.

A seventeenth I know, Bellows Verse
so that seldom shall go 162
A maiden young from me;

Long these songs thou shalt,
Loddfafnir,
Seek in vain to sing;
Yet good it were
if thou mightest get them,
Well, if thou wouldst them learn,
Help, if thou hadst them.

A seventeenth I know: Bray
so that even the shy maiden
is slow to shun my love.

These songs, Stray-Singer,
which man's son knows not,
long shall you lack in life,
though your weal
if you win them,
your boon if you obey them
your good if haply you gain them.

Verse 163

Old Norse

Þat kann ek it átjánda
er ek æva kennik
mey né manns konu
alt er betra
er einn um kann
þat fylgir ljóða lokum
nema þeiri einni
er mik armi verr
eða mín systir sé

Thorpe

For the eighteenth I know
that which I never teach
to maid or wife of man,
(all is better
what one only knows.
This is the closing of the songs)
save her alone
who clasps me in her arms,
or is my sister.

An eighteenth I know, Bellows Verse 163
that ne'er will I tell
To maiden or wife of man,--
The best is what none
but one's self doth know,
So comes the end of the songs,--
Save only to her
in whose arms I lie,
Or who else my sister is.

An eighteenth I know: Bray
which I never shall tell
to maiden or wife of man
save alone to my sister,
or haply to her
who folds me fast in her arms;
most safe are secrets
known to but one-
the songs are sung to an end.

Verse Old Nú era Háva mál kveðin
164 Norse Háva höllu í
allþörf ýta sonum
óþörf jötna sonum
heill sá er kvað
heill sá er kann
njóti sá er nam
heilir þeirs hlýddu

Thorpe Now are sung
the High-one's songs,
in the High-one's hall,
to the sons of men all-useful,
but useless to the Jotuns' sons.
Hail to him who has sung them!
Hail to him who knows them!
May he profit
who has learnt them!
Hail to those
who have heard them!

Now are Hor's words — Bellows Verse 164
spoken in the hall,
Kind for the kindred of men,
Cursed for the kindred of giants:
Hail to the speaker,
and to him who learns!
Profit be his who has them!
Hail to them who hearken!

Now the sayings of the High One — Bray
are uttered in the hall
for the weal of men,
for the woe of Jotuns,
Hail, you who have spoken!
Hail, you that knowest!
Hail, you that have hearkened!
Use, you who have learned!

## Notes

21708626R00195

Printed in Great Britain
by Amazon